ON PASSIVITY

ON PASSIVITY

A PHILOSOPHICAL DIALOGUE

Nicholas J. Pappas

Algora Publishing
New York

Library of Congress Cataloging-in-Publication Data —

Names: Pappas, Nicholas J., author.
Title: On passivity: a philosophical dialogue / Nicholas J. Pappas.
Description: New York: Algora Publishing, [2021] | Summary: "Is it always
   better to be active than passive? Is passivity a sign of cowardice - or
   prudence? Are people who keep their thoughts to themselves passive, or
   might they be actively preparing for well-considered future actions?
   Seemingly simple concepts turn out to be deeper and more significant
   than they first appear"— Provided by publisher.
Identifiers: LCCN 2020054069 (print) | LCCN 2020054070 (ebook) | ISBN
   9781628944624 (hardcover) | ISBN 9781628944617 (trade paperback) | ISBN
   9781628944631 (adobe pdf)
Subjects: LCSH: Passivity (Psychology)
Classification: LCC BF698.35.P36 P37 2021 (print) | LCC BF698.35.P36
   (ebook) | DDC 155.2/32—dc23
LC record available at https://lccn.loc.gov/2020054069
LC ebook record available at https://lccn.loc.gov/2020054070

Printed in the United States

More Books by Nick Pappas
from Algora Publishing

Controvert, or On the Lie and Other Philosophical Dialogues, 2008

Aristocrat, and The Community: Two Philosophical Dialogues, 2010

On Awareness: A Collection of Philosophical Dialogues, 2011

Belief and Integrity: Philosophical Dialogues, 2011

On Strength, 2012

On Freedom: A Philosophical Dialogue, 2014

On Life: Philosophical Dialogues, 2015

On Love: A Philosophical Dialogue, 2016

On Destiny: A Philosophical Dialogue, 2016

On Wisdom: A Philosophical Dialogue, 2017

All of Health: A Philosophical Dialogue, 2018

On Education: A Philosophical Dialogue, 2018

On Power: A Philosophical Dialogue, 2019

On Ideas: A Philosophical Dialogue, 2020

Table of Contents

INTRODUCTION   1

PART ONE. Scene: A wedding reception   3

PART TWO. Scene: The harbor   106

PART THREE. Scene: A restaurant   176

INTRODUCTION

Do you feel as though you think too much and don't act enough? Have you wondered if thinking in itself constitutes doing something? Written in dialogue format, this book explores active and passive behaviors and the relationship of each to thought.

In keeping with a long dialogic tradition, *On Passivity* encourages complex thought in the context of a simple setting. Imagining who might be a Director or how you would describe a Friend can lead to dialogue about this dialogue with your own friends.

Director and Friend, a slightly inebriated duo, meet at a wedding reception. Friend's niece was just married. Conversation between the two quickly turns to Director's pending resignation. Director is being forced to resign and Friend encourages him to resist, to take a more active role and not just accept his fate.

This exchange ignites a spark in both characters about what it means to be passive and whether it is inherently bad. Where does acceptance come into play? Director and Friend question and scrutinize many examples of passivity and activity. Hunting and fishing, thunder, cheating, friendship, love—which are passive and which are active? Why does it matter?

Director brings up the inner thoughts that drive outward behavior, and notes that "Thought is activity in the soul." Perhaps, then, it's the outer driving the inner that is passive.

How we demonstrate passivity and activity impacts how we perceive ourselves and what we learn from one another. Behaviors that appear to be passive can take significant courage. Courage is not passive.

To generate thought, the soul needs to be stirred and the thoughts expressed with others. When people demonstrate activity over passivity, this process can be described as finding: finding is a search that allows us to act on what we think in order to live a true way.

It takes many questions to sift the true and false within the active soul. You know something is true when it holds up to scrutiny. When you question and stay open to both the true and false, you reject passivity and are active.

Director and Friend question passivity throughout the wedding reception, but it doesn't end there. The search for the truth continues during a walk near the harbor. Both characters are on a quest to know. A quest to know what? Philosophy, for one thing, and maybe Life as another. They examine what philosophy is in several ways: philosophy as a love of wisdom, philosophy as a system of thought, as a mental architecture. They test and debunk the ideas about philosophy that don't hold up to scrutiny.

Director and Friend work up an appetite while discussing all their questions. The last scene takes place at a restaurant, where they disassemble and reassemble the role thought plays in gaining knowledge, reasoning, telling the truth, and living life. After digesting all this for some time, we're left with the sweet problem of rethinking everything.

Nanette F. Dunn

On Passivity

CHARACTERS: *Director, Friend*

PART ONE

SCENE: A WEDDING RECEPTION

1

Friend: But you're being so... passive!

Director: You'd rather I take a more active part in my being forced to resign?

Friend: You can fight it! You have to resist! Here, let's have another round of drinks.

Director: Tell me something. Do you distinguish between passivity and acceptance?

Friend: What do you mean?

Director: Is passivity the acceptance of all that befalls you, bad included?

Friend: I would say it is. But you can also accept only the good. And I don't think that's passive. You actively choose. So, yes. I distinguish between passivity and acceptance.

Director: What's something good that you might accept?

Friend: An award. There's nothing passive in accepting that.

Director: What if you don't want the award?

Friend: Then I suppose you might passively accept it. What's your point?

Director: If you want the award, you're not passive. If you don't want the award, you are. But the same thing happens either way. You accept the award.

Friend: Are you saying you want to be forced to resign? And don't grin like that!

Director: Sorry, I can't help but smile. It seems so crazy. If we want what we're given, we're not passive.

Friend: It seems so crazy—because it is so crazy!

Director: So we should learn to want what we're given?

Friend: You tell me.

Director: Well, tell me this. Is learning active?

Friend: Of course.

Director: So learning to want what we have is active.

Friend: You're a sophist, I see.

Director: Ha, ha.

Friend: Don't laugh. I'm serious.

Director: I know you are. Can we agree that an award and a resignation have something in common?

Friend: We can. But what do they have in common?

Director: It's very likely we did something to bring them about.

Friend: How profound.

Director: Yes. And there's more.

Friend: Pray tell.

Director: There are two types of bringing about—intentional and unintentional. Which is active and which is passive?

Friend: The intentional is active.

Director: And?

Friend: I'm not so sure about the unintentional.

Director: Why not?

Friend: Because we can be very active indeed, and have something we don't want happen.

Director: Can we be passive and bring something about?

Friend: I suppose passivity in and of itself brings certain things about.

Director: What things?

Friend: The things that come from people taking advantage of you.

Director: Why will they take advantage?

Friend: Because they can.

Director: People will do whatever they can?

Friend: They'll take advantage whenever they can.

Director: Everyone?

Friend: It's rare to find someone who won't.

Director: Which is better? To actively take advantage or to be passively taken advantage of?

Friend: Neither is better. Both are bad.

Director: If someone tries to take advantage, we should resist?

Friend: Absolutely.

Director: Am I being taken advantage of in being forced to resign?

Friend: I'm not sure.

Director: Why do you think I'm being forced to resign?

Friend: Just by being who you are you make certain people look bad.

Director: I don't look bad?

Friend: No, you don't.

Director: Isn't it a benefit not to look bad?

Friend: Sure, and your benefit is to the detriment of those who fire you.

Director: I make them look worse.

Friend: Yes.

Director: But in whose eyes?

Friend: Those who know you.

Director: The ones who are firing me don't know me?

Friend: That's a very good question. In a sense they do; in a sense they don't.

Director: If they don't know me, why would they fire me?

Friend: They think you're someone bad.

Director: Bad, or bad for them?

Friend: To them it's all the same.

Director: And if they know me, why would they fire me?

Friend: Because you really are bad for them.

Director: How so?

Friend: You shine a light on their bad deeds.

Director: Is shining light a passive affair?

Friend: No.

Director: Will their firing me shine a light on who they are?

Friend: Yes. But fighting them shines a light, too.

Director: What's the point of the fight?

Friend: To keep your job!

Director: A job where I get to work with them? Look, Friend. I did what I needed to do. And now it's time to move on.

2

Friend: So what are you trying to teach me? That certain things that seem passive aren't passive at all?

Director: Yes, but there's more to it than that. You've heard of playing the game? Well, which is more of an active thing? Playing along like everyone else, or refusing to play?

Friend: You're saying refusing to play will seem passive to some.

Director: More than some, yes. Even, and perhaps especially, to those near and dear. What happens when you refuse to play?

Friend: You pay the price.

Director: Now, and I'm not being facetious—payment is an activity. Do you agree?

Friend: I agree. To pay is a verb. But now that I say that, there are different sorts of payment.

Director: What's passive payment?

Friend: When you pay the price but do nothing about it.

Director: Do nothing? What do you mean?

Friend: You pay and pay and suffer for your payment.

Director: What else can you do?

Friend: Take steps.

Director: What steps?

Friend: You can resist.

Director: By doing what? Instead of mailing your payment in, making them come and get it?

Friend: Yes, in a sense.

Director: What else can you do?

Friend: I don't know.

Director: You can critique the game. You can tell anyone who'll listen.

Friend: What if no one listens?

Director: These things always take time. But they're helped when certain other things occur.

Friend: Like forced resignations.

Director: Things like that, sure. Everything is of a piece.

Friend: So what are you going to do? Write a tell-all book?

Director: I'll leave that to someone else.

Friend: So, what? Your life will be an open book for some author to write?

Director: No, that's not what I intend.

Friend: What do you intend?

Director: I hope to encourage others to look a little more closely at what's wrong with the game.

Friend: And by 'game' you mean business.

Director: No, I mean the game of life.

Friend: Life shouldn't be a game.

Director: Maybe. But either way, don't you think it's good to take a closer look?

Friend: Yes, yes. But we all have a front row seat at our own show.

Director: A game, a show. A game show.

Friend: Ha, ha.

Director: I think there's something important here. Games are active. We play. But shows are passive. We watch.

Friend: Not if we're all actors in the show.

Director: Okay, but then we're both active and passive. We watch the others, after all.

Friend: But we don't just watch and act. We interact.

Director: And then we're playing a game.

Friend: So what do you want from the game?

Director: I want a better game. I don't much like the one we've got.

Friend: Create a new game.

Director: Easier said than done. Games evolve over time. At best I'd like to change one of the rules.

Friend: Which rule?

Director: Well, you've got me there. I don't know.

Friend: Then how are you going to change it?

Director: You've got me again. I'm counting on others.

Friend: You'll point out where the game is flawed and hope someone else changes some rule? That's so... passive!

3

Director: You think pointing out flaws is passive? Have you ever tried to point out a flaw in something people care about?

Friend: Well....

Director: Have you ever tried to point out a flaw in something people are deeply and truly passionate about?

Friend: What's the worst that happens? They don't listen?

Director: Oh, they listen. And then, often enough, they attack.

Friend: Only if you don't let up.

Director: What's the point in pointing out flaws if you intend to let up when you meet resistance?

Friend: What kind of flaws are we talking about?

Director: Flaws in thought.

Friend: Thought. Do you know what most people think? 'I like this, and I want that.'

Director: If you like this, then why do you want that?

Friend: Oh, I'm just saying! People only care about what they like and want.

Director: Is that all you care about?

Friend: Honestly? Yes. And you?

Director: I want more of what I like and want. I'm quite active in the pursuit.

Friend: Do you succeed?

Director: Not as often as I'd like. But have you heard the saying, 'You can catch more flies with honey than vinegar'?

Friend: Yes, but I've never liked that saying.

Director: Why not?

Friend: Who wants flies?

Director: Suppose you do want flies. Is this a passive or active approach?

Friend: Well, you have to set out the honey.

Director: Yes, you have to set out the honey. And before that you have to somehow acquire the honey. That's an active pursuit.

Friend: Sure. But then you're passive as you sit and wait.

Director: Is waiting really passive? What about fishing? Active or passive?

Friend: Passive with moments of activity.

Director: Can anyone be active all the time?

Friend: Of course. Many people are.

Director: Do they get what they want?

Friend: I suppose they must. Otherwise, why be active?

Director: Suppose I'm fishing and I'm very active—I cast my line every other second.

Friend: You'll spook the fish.

Director: So I need to be more patient?

Friend: Yes.

Director: Is patience passive?

Friend: I don't really know. But I'm inclined to think it's active.

Director: Why?

Friend: Patience takes an effort.

Director: Not if you're a stone.

Friend: True, but it takes an effort when you're human. But patience can't be infinite.

Director: No, patience must have a finite purpose.

Friend: If patience has a purpose, does that mean it's not a virtue?

Director: Now why would you ask that?

Friend: Because virtues are supposed to be good for their own sake.

Director: How does that holiday song go? 'You'd better be good for goodness' sake.

Friend: Ha, ha. But seriously. Patience for the sake of patience is foolish.

Director: I agree. I'd even say it's passive.

Friend: Active virtues are for the sake of something else.

Director: Does that make them mercenary?

Friend: What are you suggesting? They're good when the pay?

Director: That's what I'm wondering. So tell me. You have a job that requires certain virtues. Are you a mercenary?

Friend: It depends.

Director: On what?

Friend: Whether I'm doing it solely for the pay.

Director: What else would you do it for?

Friend: I believe in the job. I believe in what I'm doing.

Director: What if you believe in earning pay?

Friend: Then I'm a mercenary.

Director: Mercenaries are believers?

Friend: Ha, ha. No, I wouldn't put it that way.

Director: Mercenaries don't believe.

Friend: No, mercenaries don't believe.

Director: And those who believe are... what?

Friend: Happy.

Director: Happy?

Friend: Well, maybe I should say satisfied.

Director: You can be satisfied but not happy?

Friend: Oh, what are we talking about!

Director: Being passive. Does being satisfied make you passive?

Friend: No, because you want to defend what you've got.

Director: You resist encroachments on your satisfaction.

Friend: Yes.

Director: But if there are no encroachments, you do nothing.

Friend: I suppose we can say that.

Director: So if passivity is bad, encroachments are good.

Friend: Count on you for using logic that way.

Director: What way? Who wants to be in a do-nothing torpor? Someone has to stir things up. No?

Friend: You have a point.

4

Director: But now I wonder. If someone is stirring you up, you're not being active. They are.

Friend: Once you're stirred up you have to stir yourself.

Director: Self-stirring, yes. That's clearly activity. But what if that's all you do?

Friend: What do you mean?

Director: What if you stir, and stir—but that's all you do?

Friend: If you're stirred up it will affect how you interact with others.

Director: You might stir them up, too?

Friend: Sure.

Director: And then this stirring goes on and on?

Friend: Why not?

Director: Can there be a whole nation of the stirred?

Friend: Just as there can be whole nations in torpor.

Director: But some people resist being stirred.

Friend: More than some.

Director: Why do you think they do?

Friend: They're afraid.

Director: Of what?

Friend: Motion in the soul.

Director: Are they afraid they'll lose their soul?

Friend: I think they are.

Director: How can we reassure them?

Friend: I don't think we can.

Director: Hmm. Are souls passive things?

Friend: Of course not. You can have an active soul.

Director: Then why be afraid of an active soul?

Friend: If you've never ridden a bike you're afraid you'll fall.

Director: An active soul is something you ride?

Friend: Yes, like a horse.

Director: You ride your own soul. And with a passive soul you walk.

Friend: That sounds right.

Director: What's wrong with a nation of walkers?

Friend: They don't get very far.

Director: Where can they go?

Friend: Wherever they want, so long as it's close.

Director: But what if they don't want to walk? What if there's nowhere they want to go?

Friend: Then it's too bad for them.

Director: Going somewhere is inherently good?

Friend: No, I don't know about that.

Director: So there could be a nation of stirred up devils, going heaven knows where—and it's no good.

Friend: I think that's true.

Director: Is walking really passive?

Friend: It can be active.

Director: And what if you ride something fast like a train? Active?

Friend: No, you're just riding along.

Director: To be active you have to make yourself move.

Friend: Yes. But what's the point of all this?

Director: If a nation of wasps keep stirring each other, and then they sting, are they active?

Friend: Not unless they each stir themselves. So the point is that someone can seem active—can sting—but really be passive?

Director: Yes.

Friend: How do we stir ourselves?

Director: We think.

Friend: That's ironic because we usually think of thinkers as passive. Contemplating their navel, as they say.

Director: Thinking, when it's not ruminating, stirs the soul. Because what is the soul, after all?

Friend: You should tell me.

Director: The sum of our thoughts and beliefs. How does that sound to you?

Friend: I think it's true. But what are we saying? We have to stir our beliefs? What sense does that make? Some beliefs—true beliefs—can't be stirred.

Director: If so, then the attempt at stirring makes the true clear. How does that sound?

Friend: I like it. And so the passive aren't clear on what's true in their soul. But wait. If you're stirred from outside, can you be passive and stirred at once?

Director: I think we need a distinction, one between shaken and stirred. People can shake you. But that might not make you think. You can hunker down and refuse all thought.

Friend: You cling to the false.

Director: Yes, I think that happens often. And certain people praise you by saying you're being true to your self.

Friend: 'To thine own self be true.' It should be, 'To thine true self be true.' But I don't think everyone understands the difference.

Director: No, I'm sure they don't.

Friend: We should help them.

Director: I don't know.

Friend: But isn't that what philosophy is for?

Director: Getting people to open to the truth? In part, yes.

Friend: Well, that's the most important part, whatever the rest might be. Why don't you know?

Director: Philosophy needs a spark. If there's no spark, there can't be a fire. The passive have no spark.

Friend: Give them one.

Director: I can't.

Friend: Why?

Director: Because the spark is effort. The passive make no effort. They don't try. You can't make someone try. They have to do it on their own.

Friend: But you can encourage people to try.

Director: Yes, but they have to do the trying themselves.

Friend: Then we should always encourage the passive.

Director: Yes, but for one thing. They often get annoyed with us for trying to encourage them—and sometimes they lash out.

Friend: Are you afraid of a little lashing?

Director: If it's clear no good will come of my taking abuse, I fail to see the point. Being 'active' toward no good end amounts, in my mind, to—passivity.

5

Friend: I'm not sure I buy that. The end is good, just hard to achieve. And what are you saying? Activity only comes with success?

Director: That's a good question. Maybe it's true.

Friend: You can't mean that.

Director: Why not?

Friend: You're the one who was just talking about effort! Not every effort succeeds. So are you saying you can try and be passive at once?

Director: Yes.

Friend: Ridiculous! You'd better explain.

Director: The important thing here is thought. If you try to think but fail to think, I say you're passive. Thought is activity in the soul. Failure to think is not.

Friend: Well, when you put it like that it sounds a little better. But how can you try and fail in thinking?

Director: You can think you're thinking but you're not.

Friend: What does that mean?

Director: You let ideas flit around in your head, like butterflies—or sometimes worse.

Friend: And thought is when you catch one of these butterfly ideas?

Director: Yes, something like that. The passive think that watching the butterflies fly is thought. It's not. And I think that's as far as the metaphor should go.

Friend: Why, because when you catch one, you pierce it through to affix to your collection?

Director: I'm not sure I like that image.

Friend: Ha! You have a tender heart.

Director: But do you take the point?

Friend: That you can make an effort to watch all the butterflies fly, but fail to really think, and therefore be passive? Yes, I agree.

Director: Good. These things don't admit of too much precision in speech. So if you didn't agree, I don't know if I could have convinced you.

Friend: I said I agree, not that I'm convinced.

Director: Don't do that.

Friend: What? Clarify my meaning?

Director: No. Don't agree when you don't.

Friend: But I agree for the sake of getting along.

Director: That's what I don't want.

Friend: You want to argue with me?

Director: Yes, but not as 'argue' is usually understood. Maybe 'discuss', or 'converse', or 'engage' is better. So why aren't you convinced?

Friend: Because you don't say what you do when the idea is caught.

Director: You examine it closely.

Friend: And then?

Director: You decide if it should stay in your soul.

Friend: And if not, you open your soul and let it fly away?

Director: Yes.

Friend: And if it should stay in your soul?

Director: You let it go back with the others. But here's the important thing. Now you know it for what it is. So when you look at the ideas in your soul, you'll always recognize this idea as special, as one you truly know.

Friend: And the notion is to truly know all the ideas in your soul.

Director: Yes. And that's the work of a lifetime.

Friend: It's active work.

Director: Highly.

Friend: Well, now I'm convinced.

Director: Good.

6

Friend: But you're focused wholly on inner activity. We have to acknowledge outer activity, too.

Director: They are one. Name an outer activity.

Friend: Resisting a call to resign.

Director: How would someone do that?

Friend: They need the nerve to tell the boss they won't resign.

Director: Do they use words to do this?

Friend: Of course.

Director: Where do words come from?

Friend: The mouth.

Director: Where does the mouth get the words?

Friend: You want me to say from the mind or soul.

Director: It's true, isn't it? That's where we find our words. Mind, soul, brain— there are many ways to describe it, but it's all the same thing. The inner drives the outer.

Friend: Sometimes the outer drives the inner.

Director: Maybe when you're passive, sure. Or do you think it's active to be driven so?

Friend: No, you have a point. So it's drive or be driven in this world. Be active or passive, with nothing between.

Director: Oh, there's plenty between. Who is perfectly one or the other? No one. So all I can say is this. When we feel we're driven, we have to step back and drive.

Friend: We have to try, try to step back and drive.

Director: Did you think we can do it without trying?

Friend: Of course not. But what if we can't step back? Life doesn't always give us that choice.

Director: How passive. When life doesn't give, we must take.

Friend: Take back the helm?

Director: Yes. We must actively steer and not just drift.

Friend: Steer away from trouble, you mean.

Director: And toward what we want.

Friend: What does it mean to steer?

Director: To say the things that count.

Friend: 'I will not resign,' for one.

Director: That's one way to go. 'I will resign,' is another.

Friend: You really want to resign?

Director: I do.

Friend: But you're being forced.

Director: Is it bad to be forced to do what you want? Besides, who brought things to this head?

Friend: You did?

Director: I did. I was steering this way for a while.

Friend: I don't understand. Why not just quit?

Director: The reasons for that are mine. And that's another part of being active. You keep certain things to yourself.

Friend: Keeping seems passive to me.

Director: Not when it's easier to share.

Friend: And if it's harder to share?

Director: You raise an interesting point. Is the active always the harder? That may be.

Friend: So we should always do what's harder. It was harder for you to resign?

Director: Yes. Well, then again... maybe.

Friend: Ha! You're not sure?

Director: How can I be sure? Maybe it would be harder to stay. But I don't like where we're headed. It's harder to walk on burning coals than it is to walk on grass—at least I think it is. Should we always walk on burning coals?

Friend: Yes, I know what you mean. Harder isn't always better. So how do we know what's better?

Director: 'Better' as in more active? Or can passivity be better at times?

Friend: Don't you think it's always better to think? Isn't that the standard of activity?

Director: Now I'm not so sure.

Friend: Why not?

Director: It's common knowledge that passive is bad. But what if passive is good?

Friend: Impossible. How could that be?

7

Director: What if being passive allows you to see?

Friend: See the butterfly ideas in our heads?

Director: Sure, but others' butterflies, too.

Friend: What good does seeing them do?

Director: Maybe sight is its own good. There's pleasure in sight. And we learn from what we see. Sight can satisfy our urge to know. Sight can help us when we're active.

Friend: Passivity for activity?

Director: Yes, why not? But what about activity for passivity?

Friend: How would that work?

Director: In order to see we have to be in proper position. Getting there takes effort.

Friend: I like that.

Director: Sometimes there are mountains to climb, deserts to cross, oceans to travel—all before we can see.

Friend: Yes, and when you arrive, if you're active, you might disturb the natural picture.

Director: We must lie in wait, like hunters—and then we catch our prey through sight.

Friend: But then we act on what we see.

Director: Yes, so it's activity for the sake of the passive; then passivity for the sake of the active. Neither has precedence over the other. They work together as peers.

Friend: I never thought I'd agree to something like that, but I'm convinced.

Director: Yes, but now I have doubts.

Friend: About what?

Director: Sight.

Friend: What's to doubt about sight? You just sit back and see.

Director: But that's what I doubt. Sight might have to be active in order to be good.

Friend: Good? Seeing is good, active or passive. But why active?

Director: So you can make sense of what you see.

Friend: And how do you do that?

Director: You reason as you see.

Friend: Reason about what you're watching?

Director: Yes. And here's something I don't think you'll like.

Friend: What?

Director: Some people are born to reason; others are not.

Friend: That's ridiculous. You mean to say if I see something my brain might just shut down; but you, you will see the same thing and your brain will light up with activity?

Director: Yes. And maybe it differs with different things. My brain might light for one thing, and your brain might light for another.

Friend: I guess I can see some truth in that. But if you can't help yourself, is that really active?

Director: Many of us have to help ourselves—because we have an impulse to stifle our thought.

Friend: But then the stifling is the activity, and thought—thought just happens!

Director: No, Friend. We must resist the impulse. So it's activity, resistance, for the sake of activity, thought.

Friend: Sounds tiring. But I'm of the opinion we just let go and let thought happen.

Director: And maybe that's how an important part of thought works.

Friend: Which part?

Director: Maybe the beginning. Or is it the end? I don't know.

Friend: I think we need another drink. Bartender! I hate weddings.

Director: Why? This one is nice.

Friend: Yes, yes. Nice.

Director: Your niece looks lovely.

Friend: She always looks lovely.

Director: She looks happy.

Friend: How long do you think that will last?

Director: A lifetime?

Friend: Ha! With that guy?

Director: What's wrong with him?

Friend: He's too... nice!

Director: Too nice for your liking?

Friend: Yes. Give me someone with more... sand.

Director: Grit?

Friend: Grit.

Director: But your niece wants nice.

Friend: Well, bless her—she's got it.

8

Director: What's wrong with nice?

Friend: It's passive. 'Nice' goes along to get along.

Director: You'd rather he didn't get along?

Friend: You don't get along. Neither do I.

Director: No one's asking you to resign. Oh, I'm teasing. Don't get upset.

Friend: I'm always a word or two away from being asked. You know this.

Director: I know this. Do you want your nephew-in-law to be a word or two away?

Friend: Maybe not that close—but closer.

Director: Closer. Closer to the truth?

Friend: Exactly! The truth is dangerous. You and I are very close. I'd be happy if he could understand what this means.

Director: What does it mean?

Friend: You have to be on guard.

Director: Oh, I think the nice are on guard.

Friend: On guard from what?

Director: Seeming mean.

Friend: I don't think he has it in him.

Director: Probe and see.

Friend: And risk falling out with my niece?

Director: No, you're right. You should be nice to your niece, and all that is hers. In fact, you should be nice to all those related to you, and all that is theirs. And, in fact—

Friend: Oh, shut up.

Director: I was going to say you should be nice to your friends.

Friend: You should be honest with your friends.

Director: You think 'nice' and 'honest' don't go together?

Friend: Of course they don't! The nice avoid honesty like the plague.

Director: Why?

Friend: Nothing ruffles feathers like honesty.

Director: So being honest is never passive. To ruffle is an act.

Friend: To ruffle is an act. Agreed.

Director: And if I avoid an arrow to my heart, is that an act?

Friend: What are you talking about?

Director: You said the passive avoid honesty. I'd like to know if avoidance is ever an act.

Friend: Yes, yes. Strictly speaking, it's an act.

Director: So avoiding honesty isn't passive? What's wrong? Going passive on me now?

Friend: Avoidance is an act.

Director: But you feel it's a passive act.

Friend: I do.

Director: If there are passive actions, are there active passivities?

Friend: Why not?

Director: Yes. Can you give an example of one?

Friend: We just gave one. You actively avoid the truth.

Director: Hmm. I'm not sure about all this.

Friend: I know what you mean. My head is starting to hurt.

Director: Better cut back on the drinks.

Friend: Ha, ha. I see you're holding your own.

Director: I almost always do. Is holding your own active or passive?

Friend: Active.

Director: How so?

Friend: You actively develop your tolerance.

Director: And what about my tolerance for others?

Friend: Same thing. Active development.

Director: And once it's developed? Passive enjoyment?

Friend: I suppose you have a point. Sure, passive enjoyment—assuming it's enjoyable to tolerate others.

Director: I think it is, if we're talking about true tolerance. But what about holding your own in another sense, the sense of being able to stand your ground with others?

Friend: That is definitely active.

Director: Even if you're just... standing there?

Friend: Hmm. First, you have to claim the ground you want to make your own. Then you make it your own. Then you stand that ground. Two parts active, one part passive?

Director: That's how it seems to me. And maybe that's how it is in all things in life.

Friend: Yes, but now I see we've forgotten something. When you stand your ground, people are trying to push you off of it. Your resistance to them has to be active.

Director: Ah, a good point. But what are we talking about?

Friend: What do you mean? You tell me.

Director: Conversation. You stand your ground in conversation. That means you don't budge. What does it mean not to budge, not to budge in what you say?

Friend: You stand by your words.

Director: Are words active or passive?

Friend: Words are... active! They have to be.

Director: Why do they have to be?

Friend: Because words have power.

Director: And there's no such thing as passive power? In other words, is power always active?

Friend: Well, I suppose power could be dormant. But it's active when it's used.

Director: If I'm a tyrant, and I want a man dead, all I have to do is nod to one of my slaves and the deed will be done. Active?

Friend: Yes.

Director: A nod of the head? That's very little activity, if you ask me.

Friend: Yes, but that nod is the culmination of years of struggle for power.

Director: But we're not talking about the struggle. We're talking about the nod and only the nod.

Friend: The nod is passive.

Director: Even if lots of thought went into the nod?

Friend: Tyrants don't think.

Director: Really? How do they stay in power?

Friend: Which side of the issue are you on?

Director: I'm trying to figure that out. So how is it? Do tyrants think?

Friend: Oh, everyone thinks, if only a little.

Director: And we agree that thinking is active?

Friend: We agree.

Director: Then the thought that goes into staying in power must be active.

Friend: It must.

Director: But the deeds that issue from that thought—the nods, so to speak—can be passive?

Friend: I suppose they can. But they'd be active if the tyrant did them him or herself.

9

Director: Maybe that's the thing!

Friend: What thing?

Director: The difference between doing things yourself and having others do them. The one is active the other is passive.

Friend: I like that definition.

Director: But then there's a difficulty. All great leaders, throughout all of history, were more passive than active.

Friend: Because they couldn't have done most of what they did on their own?

Director: Yes. What do you think?

Friend: Generals have armies. They command their armies to do certain things. But can we really say command is passive?

Director: Command might have different components, active and passive. Maybe the active comes through those they deal with directly; and the passive is the indirect, down the chain of command.

Friend: I don't know. Maybe. But does this hold for others than leaders?

Director: Sure. A certain author might suggest certain things that lead to certain actions by certain others.

Friend: That's a lot of certainty.

Director: Yes. But what do you think? Passive?

Friend: Probably. But I'd say that author is a leader.

Director: What's the best an author can do to avoid being passive?

Friend: Model the behavior they want to see in others.

Director: Role models aren't passive?

Friend: Of course not.

Director: How about fashion models?

Friend: Ha, ha.

Director: And what about the tyrant?

Friend: The tyrant is probably a very good role model for those who would kill.

Director: So when the tyrant nods it's not passive?

Friend: No, I think it's still passive but to a lesser degree.

Director: Hmm. Did those who asked me to resign nod?

Friend: You know they did. They wanted you to take the action they wouldn't.

Director: Some would say they're doing me a favor.

Friend: Some favor. Everyone knows what's going on.

Director: So no one can ever simply resign? Everyone will know what's going on?

Friend: That's their trap. You can't win.

Director: Traps are passive, no?

Friend: Traps are very passive, yes.

Director: Trappers are passive while hunters are active?

Friend: I think that's fair to say.

Director: A hunter would fire me, out and out.

Friend: That's right. A hunter has more guts. The hunter must do the killing. A trapper lets the trap kill the prey—slowly.

Director: Better to die all at once, rather than rot in some trap.

Friend: That's my preference, yes. And yours?

Director: Better to die all at once. So we have to steer clear of traps.

Friend: Ha! You've just trapped yourself!

Director: I have? How?

Friend: Your resignation is a trap. Refuse to resign and force them to kill you all at once.

Director: But if I sign the resignation I'm killed at once. It appears some traps are designed to kill with mercy.

Friend: Oh, don't give me that! There's no mercy here. They want to fire you indirectly. Force them to take the direct step.

Director: Why? What difference does it make? If I resign I have plausibility for when I seek another job.

Friend: Well, if you want a job based on plausibility, by all means resign.

Director: I'll need another job, you know. It's harder to find one when you're fired. I have to be practical.

Friend: And being practical is active?

Director: I think it often is.

Friend: Is being impractical passive?

Director: Not always, no. But it can be.

Friend: Can being practical be passive?

Director: Well, you raise an interesting question. I think the answer is yes.

10

Friend: How?

Director: Put simply, it might be practical to go with the flow.

Friend: And when we go with the flow we're passive.

Director: If we let ourselves go? Yes.

Friend: What if we don't let ourselves go?

Director: We might swim to the head of the flow—in order to change its direction.

Friend: That sounds like a risky affair.

Director: That's why it's active.

Friend: Interesting. Is activity always associated with risk?

Director: Thinking, for one, always involves a risk.

Friend: What risk?

Director: You might not accept the thought.

Friend: What happens when you don't accept a thought?

Director: You get sick.

Friend: Thought sickness?

Director: Thought sickness indeed.

Friend: 'In-deed'? Does accepting a thought mean to act on it?

Director: What else would you do with a thought? Contemplate it in all passive glory?

Friend: No, we have to act on our thoughts. We have to have guts.

Director: 'Guts' translate thoughts to action?

Friend: What else would?

Director: I don't know. But I'm struck by something. Guts is plural.

Friend: So?

Director: We say, 'I trust my gut.' But 'we have to have guts'. Why do we trust the singular but act on the plural?

Friend: Now you're quibbling.

Director: Am I? I think there's truth to be found in words, in language. Can't we look for it here?

Friend: I suppose we can trust our guts, and that we have to have gut.

Director: So there's really no difference?

Friend: No, I don't think there is.

Director: The singular and plural are interchangeable.

Friend: And what do you think that goes to show?

Director: That we don't really know what our gut is.

Friend: We rely on and trust something we don't know?

Director: Yes. I think we make a sort of leap of faith.

Friend: Is this faith active or passive?

Director: What do you think?

Friend: I think faith is different. It's an enabler.

Director: What does it enable?

Friend: Action.

Director: Faith enables thought?

Friend: Oh, I'm not talking about thought. I'm talking about action—real action.

Director: One word about faith and thought is reduced to unreal action.

Friend: We have to think, then act. And thought tells us what to believe.

Director: Thought gives us faith?

Friend: Exactly. And then we act on our faith.

Director: Why not act on our thought?

Friend: Thought is frail. Faith is firm.

Director: Thought can be firm—when we stand our ground.

Friend: Yes, yes. But it's easier to stand firm with faith.

Director: Once we stand firm, do we always stand firm?

Friend: What do you mean?

Director: Do we ever shift our ground?

Friend: Are we ever shifty?

Director: 'Shifty' implies we shift all the time. I'm talking about a considered shift.

Friend: Sure, sometimes we shift.

Director: Would faith get in the way of such a shift?

Friend: It might.

Director: How do we persuade faith to shift, assuming a shift is in order?

Friend: It's not easy.

Director: Why not?

Friend: Because faith, once set, doesn't listen.

Director: We can't reason with faith?

Friend: Not very well.

Director: Then how do we persuade faith to shift?

Friend: We need to articulate a new faith, one more appealing.

Director: That doesn't sound very easy.

Friend: No, it's not. Only the rarest of individuals can articulate a new faith.

Director: I thought we come up with faith on our own.

Friend: Yes, and no. We have our own personal faith, informed by the faith of the great leaders.

Director: Hmm. You said faith is different, that it's an enabler, and therefore not active or passive. But I'm not so sure about that. So humor me a bit.

Friend: How shall I humor you?

Director: Tell me, even if you're not sure. Is personal faith active and the larger faith passive? Or is it the other way round? Or is all faith active? Or passive?

Friend: Faith is not so easily reduced.

Director: Can we at least say some faith is active and some is passive?

Friend: I think that's all we can say.

11

Director: What makes faith active? Without that, we must say it's passive. No?

Friend: Faith that makes us think is active. How's that?

Director: Not too bad. What's an example?

Friend: Faith in yourself.

Director: How does that make you think?

Friend: With each situation you find yourself in, you believe that you can succeed. But you have to think how.

Director: You believe that if you think, and think very well, you'll succeed.

Friend: Yes.

Director: I think I like your active faith. And I take it that if you believe you'll succeed but don't think how, your faith is passive?

Friend: What else could it be?

Director: You have a point. So thinking and faith can go together.

Friend: Did you have any doubt?

Director: I did. But now I'm inclined to see how they help each other.

Friend: How thinking helps faith is obvious. But how does faith help thinking?

Director: I'm not entirely sure.

Friend: Well, I'll tell you. To think, we need some ground to stand on. Faith gives us that ground.

Director: Hmm.

Friend: What's wrong?

Director: Why can't thinking give us the ground? Or better, maybe we get our ground through luck.

Friend: What kind of luck?

Director: The luck of where we're thrown in the world. We take what we find and accept it as our own.

Friend: What's this? 'Bloom where you're planted'?

Director: Call it what you like. I think it's where we find our ground.

Friend: And then we claim more.

Director: We certainly can. But some people need only a small bit of this sort of ground.

Friend: Why not have as much ground as you can?

Director: Thought only needs a little. And thought is, after all, what we're about.

Friend: Because the more you think the more active you are.

Director: Yes, but let's not disparage small, active steps. They are as much activity as great big bounds.

Friend: Tell me something, Director. We spoke of nods. But what about shaking your head?

Director: What about it?

Friend: Is it harder to shake or nod? To say no or yes?

Director: To go along or resist? Is that what you're asking?

Friend: I am.

Director: I think it's harder to resist. But everyone might be saying no, and then you nod yes. That's a kind of resistance, isn't it?

Friend: Of course it is.

Director: And is that what resistance is? Going against all the others?

Friend: What else would it be?

Director: Maybe only one of the others pressures you. You resist against one while many look on.

Friend: That's resistance, no doubt—and difficult, too, because of those looking on.

Director: But the lookers-on are passive, no?

Friend: I think they are.

Director: Can the passive lend support to those who pressure?

Friend: They can. They're passively complicit in this.

Director: And if complicit, guilty?

Friend: Guilty as sin.

12

Director: Which is worse? To be actively guilty or passively guilty?

Friend: It makes no difference. Guilt is guilt.

Director: Who is more likely to reform?

Friend: I don't know.

Director: You surprise me. I thought you would say the passive.

Friend: Why?

Director: Because the passive aren't in as deep. They haven't thought things through.

Friend: Let me tell you something. Sometimes the active are shallow and the passive are deep. In fact, that's how I think it usually is.

Director: Why passive and deep?

Friend: If you're in the water, and you do nothing, you sink.

Director: What about the dead man's float?

Friend: Oh, you know what I mean. The passive sink—they go deep.

Director: And the active are on the surface of things?

Friend: More often than not? Yes. The surface is where the action is, and should be.

Director: Why?

Friend: So we can all see just what goes on.

Director: See as in passively see?

Friend: No! See as in prepare to do something about it.

Director: Make things better, you mean.

Friend: Yes, of course.

Director: And only the active can make something better?

Friend: The passive certainly can't.

Director: Why not?

Friend: They don't care.

Director: What do you mean?

Friend: The passive are lazy. And the lazy care only about themselves, not making things better for all.

Director: Ah, for all. And the active care about all?

Friend: It's not that simple. Being active gives you the capacity to care about others.

Director: But we can have the capacity and not care. What makes the difference here?

Friend: Desire.

Director: Desire for what?

Friend: Admiration and praise.

Director: The passive don't care about that?

Friend: They really don't.

Director: Praise is a spur.

Friend: The finest spur there is.

Director: And it only works on the active.

Friend: Do you have any doubt?

Director: None to speak of. Too bad we can't find a way to spur the passive. But maybe....

Friend: Maybe what?

Director: Maybe the passive can be spurred if only they're well enough known to...

Friend: To whom?

Director: ...a philosopher.

13

Friend: What can a philosopher do?

Director: Examine the passive soul and find where there might be sparks.

Friend: And then light the soul aflame?

Director: A philosopher can encourage a spark, but the soul must spark itself and light itself aflame.

Friend: And then the passive will care for others?

Director: There's a decent chance. But it will be others like themselves.

Friend: Well, I suppose that's an improvement.

Director: Don't we all care for others like ourselves? Even the highly active?

Friend: The highly active should care for all.

Director: Maybe then they'd be too 'active'.

Friend: No, it's good to care for all. It's noble to care for others unlike ourselves.

Director: Others like the bad?

Friend: Sure, others like the bad. It's easy to care for those like us. It's hard to care for the different. Don't you know about the value of diversity?

Director: But how can we care for the different? Don't we have to know them in order to care, actively care? Or is simple caring from the heart enough?

Friend: Caring from the heart is a start. But yes, you're right. We have to know them in order to help. Otherwise we might think we're helping when we're not.

Director: And it's easy to know those like us?

Friend: Well, that assumes we know ourselves.

Director: True. And if we don't?

Friend: We'll make the same mistakes on them we make on ourselves.

Director: Getting to know yourself is active?

Friend: Yes.

Director: Once you know yourself, is knowing yourself active?

Friend: No, I don't think it is.

Director: It's passive?

Friend: Maybe it's something between.

Director: Fair enough. But if knowing yourself is something between, is knowing others like you the same?

Friend: In between? I think it has to be.

Director: But getting to know unlike-others is active.

Friend: Yes.

Director: And when we know them—the fact of knowing them—that's something between?

Friend: I suppose it is.

Director: But if we try to change them, that's an active thing.

Friend: Of course it is.

Director: And leaving them alone is passive.

Friend: Right.

Director: Is it always good to try to change someone?

Friend: No, not always.

Director: Because it assumes we know better?

Friend: Sometimes we do know better.

Director: How do we know we know better?

Friend: We prove it through reasoning with them.

Director: Ah, reason. A great activity. Never passive.

Friend: Never say never.

Director: How is reason passive?

Friend: When you're just chewing the cud.

Director: That's not reason. Reason always has something at stake. There's risk in reason, as we've suggested. When you have a conversation with a friend, and you think you know better—isn't something at stake?

Friend: Of course there is.

Director: What?

Friend: You might be wrong.

Director: What happens then?

Friend: You might lose your friend.

Director: And if you're right?

Friend: You still might lose your friend—or you might help.

Director: Friendship and/or betterment is at stake.

Friend: Yes. But have we just defined the active? The active always has something at stake. The passive has nothing.

Director: That may well be the definition that sticks. But what about the tyrant's passive nod? Isn't there something important at stake?

Friend: Not for the tyrant, not really. He or she will still be in power. Sure, the murder might set in motion a chain of events that brings the tyrant down—it might be the straw that breaks the camel's back—but there are a lot of straws before that point, if it ever comes.

Director: Meanwhile the camel passively allows straw after straw.

Friend: Yes. Who can refuse such a little straw and not seem unreasonable?

Director: Someone with principles?

Friend: Exactly that! A camel with principles refuses the straw! Each and every straw!

Director: And camels with principles are... usually out of work.

14

Friend: Don't be so negative. They can refuse when they know they're close to their limit.

Director: Then the principle is, 'Passively accept—until you must actively resist.' But what if then it's too late? 'A million straws have passed, and now you say no? Just one more, Mr. Camel. Please?'

Friend: Yes, yes. That undoubtedly happens. But the camel must refuse.

Director: Or have an owner that actively looks to its interest.

Friend: But the owner will have the same problem.

Director: Not if the owner has a scale. 'Only so much weight—exactly so, with no exceptions—and then no more.' That works, doesn't it?

Friend: That works well.

Director: So what's the principle here?

Friend: The principle is making no exceptions—ever.

Director: And if a camel owner comes along with a camel who can bear a pound more?

Friend: We stick to our principle.

Director: But what if we're wrong? What if our camel can handle five pounds more?

Friend: Well, that's the trick. We have to know the limit, know it exactly so.

Director: How do we arrive at knowledge of the limit?

Friend: Through experience.

Director: Through going until we break our camel's back?

Friend: No, of course not. We look for suffering.

Director: We don't want our camel to suffer. But you know the problem. What if our camel is a little too... sensitive?

Friend: Well yes, that complicates things.

Director: And what if our camel is a touch... lazy.

Friend: Complications again.

Director: So how do we know the limit?

Friend: We have to use our expert judgement.

Director: We have to be good judges of camel character?

Friend: Ha, ha. Yes.

Director: And only time, and the health of our camel, will tell.

Friend: Right. And in the meantime we're strict.

Director: Right or wrong we're strict. And it's active to be strict?

Friend: Don't tell me you think it's passive.

Director: Well, if we're strict without thought...

Friend: ...then the Nazis were passive.

Director: That's quite a leap to make. But I'm inclined to agree. There's nothing active in 'just following orders'.

Friend: But their atrocities were active.

Director: No, they were passive, too. A tragedy of the passive. If only someone had stood forth and acted in truth.

Friend: Now I see what you mean. There was no internal resistance—or not enough.

Director: Not enough, no. Maybe they were blinded by all the external activity.

Friend: There might be something to that, yes. But really, Director, I'm having a hard time. Common sense says the Nazis weren't passive.

Director: They were passive aggressive?

Friend: Ha! I don't think they were that.

Director: Not in the generally accepted sense of that phrase, no. But in our sense? I think they may have been. Remember, there was no thought.

Friend: But there was thought behind what they did.

Director: Was there?

Friend: Ideology.

Director: Would you agree that to follow an ideology is passive?

Friend: I can agree to that. But to create an ideology, that's an act.

Director: A good act or a bad act?

Friend: A bad act.

Director: Because the act leads to passive following?

Friend: Of course.

Director: Can we generalize? Activity that leads to passivity is bad.

Friend: Yes.

Director: And activity that leads to activity is good?

Friend: No doubt.

Director: What about passivity that leads to passivity?

Friend: You know it's bad.

Director: Then tell me what I don't know. What about passivity that leads to activity?

Friend: You'll have to give me an example.

Director: I can't. But I think it's at least somewhat good.

Friend: But passivity can't 'lead' anywhere. It doesn't lead. It just is. So nothing follows from it. Which means it can't take credit for the activity that comes after it in time. Chronology isn't causality. In fact, there may have been more activity if not for the passivity.

Director: I see you feel strongly about this. Well, you have a point.

Friend: There's no such thing as passivity that leads to activity. That's my point.

Director: Then is there really such a thing as activity that leads to passivity? Let's take ideology. Is its creation truly active?

Friend: Why wouldn't it be? Thought goes into it.

Director: Thought, or the mechanical assembly of certain ideas?

Friend: Well, when you put it like that.... But isn't assembly active? Common sense says it is.

Director: Is disassembly active?

Friend: Sure, as active as assembly. Why?

Director: Why is it active?

Friend: It takes thought to tease ideas apart.

Director: As much thought as it takes to weave ideas together?

Friend: Weave them into a fabric, sure. We need these fabrics in order to clothe ourselves, you know.

Director: Then why would we strip ourselves naked?

Friend: Who says we would?

Director: Isn't that what we do when we tease the ideas apart? Or do we strip others and remain fully clothed ourselves?

Friend: I think this talk of stripping has to stop.

Director: Then let's get back to the point. Clothing another is active.

Friend: Yes.

Director: When the other is clothed, as far as clothing goes, there's nothing more to do. Or am I missing something?

Friend: No, you're not missing anything.

Director: The nothing-more-to-do is passive. Yes?

Friend: It's passive.

Director: Then there is activity that leads to passivity. So it's bad to clothe people.

Friend: Now you're being ridiculous.

Director: Wouldn't it be better to teach them how to weave and sew?

Friend: There's truth in that, but it's impractical.

Director: Maybe we're missing something. Maybe people really aren't passive when we make them clothes.

Friend: What do they do?

Director: If the clothes are right, they cavort.

Friend: Cavort? Ha, ha! True! I'll take your point—though it seems to me you had to stretch and cheat to make it.

Director: Stretch and cheat? Isn't it better to do that than be passive and fail to make a point?

Friend: Without a doubt.

15

Director: When do you stretch and cheat, Friend?

Friend: If you don't know, why would I tell you?

Director: Can you stretch and cheat and not be aware that's what you're doing?

Friend: I suppose.

Director: In that case are you actively stretching and cheating?

Friend: Maybe not.

Director: Regardless, if we see someone doing this, should we just passively accept it?

Friend: No, of course not. We must call them on it. We must actively resist.

Director: Even if that gets us into trouble?

Friend: Even so.

Director: What if we just refuse to go along?

Friend: That's a kind of resistance. Say nothing but stand your ground.

Director: And if because of that your boss asks you to resign?

Friend: That's what happened to you?

Director: In part.

Friend: What was the other part?

Director: When asked, I explained why I was resisting.

Friend: Ha! That must have gone over well. So you told him he was cheating?

Director: I did.

Friend: What was he doing? One set of rules for himself and another for the others?

Director: He was doing that. But that wasn't my problem. I told him he wasn't engaging.

Friend: Being active?

Director: Yes. He was running around making all kinds of noise but in fact was doing nothing.

Friend: And you told him this.

Director: I told him this.

Friend: Explain it to me. How was that cheating?

Director: He wanted something to come of nothing. And he penalized people when nothing came.

Friend: To penalize like that is to cheat?

Director: I think it is. Don't you?

Friend: I don't know. I've never looked at it that way before. Cheating means to break the rules. What rule did he break?

Director: That you should only be penalized for things within your control.

Friend: Yes, I think I see what you mean. But things start to get murky here.

Director: Passivity generates murk.

Friend: And activity clears it up?

Director: Yes. But only true activity.

Friend: And that truth is thought.

Director: Thought and acting on what we think.

Friend: Ah, that's the trick. We have to be true to what we think.

Director: That's the only worthwhile act in the world. We must do justice to our thought.

Friend: And if our thought isn't right?

Director: Part of doing justice is making it right. We learn, an activity, then act on what we learn.

Friend: What's the difference between thinking and learning?

Director: Maybe nothing. We learn when we think. Otherwise, what's the point of thought?

Friend: But we can learn what's true or learn what's false.

Director: It's thought and learning either way.

Friend: So you can learn from those who cheat.

Director: Yes. Just as you can learn from those who play by the rules.

Friend: You can learn from everyone?

Director: Except from those who refuse to play.

Friend: What does it mean not to play? And why can't we learn from those who don't?

Director: Let's drop the game metaphor and take this head on. We have nothing to learn from those who don't think.

Friend: But we can learn what it means not to think.

Director: Okay. But we learn this once and then we know. Everyone who doesn't think is the same. Do you agree?

Friend: I agree. They're the same in the only thing that counts.

Director: Now, there are those who think well. And we can surely learn from them.

Friend: Surely.

Director: And there are those who almost think well. I hold that we can learn from them, too.

Friend: So do I.

Director: What can we learn?

Friend: What not to do.

Director: And what can we learn from those who think well?

Friend: We can learn what to do.

Director: If we have knowledge of both what to do and what not to do, is our knowledge complete?

Friend: What else is there to learn?

Director: I don't know. But let's be open to the possibility that there might be something more.

16

Friend: We can be open, sure. But we've covered the gamut.

Director: Which gamut?

Friend: The active and passive! Knowing what to do and doing it is active; knowing what not to do and not doing it is passive.

Director: I don't know, Friend.

Friend: What now?

Director: I agree that knowing what to do and doing it is active; but I'm inclined to think knowing what not to do and not doing it, too, is active.

Friend: How can not doing be active?

Director: Not doing based on ignorance is passive. But it's the knowledge that matters. The knowledge guides us. Guiding is active, a verb—even if it guides us to do nothing.

Friend: Let me guess. Your knowledge is guiding you to do nothing concerning your resignation.

Director: It's a bit more complicated than that. But essentially? Yes.

Friend: Okay. But I think there's a problem here, though I'm not sure how to explain. If we guide ourselves, I can see that's active. But what if something else guides us? Do you know what I mean?

Director: I think I do. And I'd explain it like this. If the knowledge that guides us is our own, we're active. But if the knowledge is other, is from outside—passive.

Friend: Exactly.

Director: So, to be active, knowledge must be us, must be ourselves.

Friend: Knowledge can't be other, yes.

Director: We must be our knowledge. But is this 'being' active or passive?

Friend: I'm going to say something crazy.

Director: That's alright. We can blame it on the drinks.

Friend: Being must be active. Because if you passively 'be', you really don't exist.

Director: The passive doesn't exist?

Friend: Not in any real sense, not when it comes to being.

Director: How many passive people do you think are in the world?

Friend: Many.

Director: So what are they? So many walking dead?

Friend: Precisely.

Director: And that's because their knowledge isn't themselves. Their knowledge is other. It's some external force.

Friend: Yes, I like that. External force. Their knowledge is from without.

Director: But the living, the active, have their knowledge within.

Friend: They incorporate their knowledge into their soul. And then their soul guides them.

Director: This is all fairly profound.

Friend: But true?

Director: I think there's truth in what we're saying. But what does it mean for knowledge to be from without?

Friend: It comes from others.

Director: So if you take your knowledge from me somehow, you're passive.

Friend: Right.

Director: What if you take it from me and then incorporate it into your soul?

Friend: Well....

Director: And does it matter if my knowledge is from within or without?

Friend: I think we have to distinguish between 'knowledge' and knowledge.

Director: Ah. So if I give you 'knowledge', you can't help but be passive with it?

Friend: Yes. And if you give me knowledge, true knowledge, it's active with you and then active with me—assuming I incorporate it into my soul.

Director: What happens if you incorporate 'knowledge' into your soul?

Friend: You ruin your soul.

Director: So it's vital to know the difference between 'knowledge' and knowledge.

Friend: Yes. So how can we tell?

Director: It's simple. False knowledge isn't true.

Friend: What makes something true?

Director: Oh, you're asking a very big question.

Friend: We have time.

Director: Alright. Let's start with something simple. The true holds up when questioned.

Friend: But the false holds up when questioned—questioned not very well.

Director: Then let's say the true holds up when questioned, questioned as well as can be.

Friend: How do we know it's as well as can be?

Director: We must exhaust every possibility.

Friend: How do we know what's possible?

Director: We have to be open, and not assume we know. But, Friend, there's something important here.

Friend: What?

Director: We have to be very, very patient—when we hope to know.

17

Friend: The passive aren't patient.

Director: Not at all.

Friend: But that seems counter to common sense. The passive have nothing but time on their hands.

Director: Do they? I sometimes think the passive are rushed. They don't have time to learn.

Friend: Why don't they have time?

Director: They're very busy being passive.

Friend: But how?

Director: The external presses on them. And they must press back.

Friend: That's not very passive. But they're right about one thing—we must resist the external.

Director: Yes, but there's a danger here. When we resist we have to somehow stay open to things that are true.

Friend: Of course. But how do we know what's true? How do we know to open up?

Director: I think you're going to doubt me here.

Friend: Why?

Director: Because we have to stay open to all.

Friend: Even the false?

Director: Even the false.

Friend: But that's ridiculous! Why be open to something we know is false?

Director: Because it might prove to be true.

Friend: We'll be overwhelmed!

Director: No. The false will gain no purchase in our soul. If the false is passive, how can it overrun an active soul?

Friend: You have a point. But then we're always sifting the true from the false.

Director: Yes. That's part of having an active soul.

Friend: Is there no rest?

Director: There is no rest for the wicked. But, fortunately, we're not wicked, my friend.

Friend: Ha, ha. But really, is there no rest?

Director: Haven't you ever heard people say, 'I'll rest when I die'?

Friend: I have. But I always thought they were wrong-headed here.

Director: Well, we can rest when alive—because we're not afraid of what the false and passive can do.

Friend: What can't they do?

Director: Invade our souls and steal our knowledge away.

Friend: Why can't they do that?

Director: Because they'd have to kill us to succeed.

Friend: Destroy our soul? But that's possible, isn't it?

Director: Only we can destroy our own soul.

Friend: We're the architects of our destruction?

Director: The sole and only true architect, yes.

Friend: How do we destroy our soul?

Director: By making false knowledge 'true'.

Friend: By embracing the false?

Director: By making the false our own.

Friend: So we have some affinity to the false?

Director: Yes.

Friend: But then what is this? Predestination?

Director: Call it what you will.

Friend: Some people are born for the false, and some people are born for the true?

Director: It often seems that way to me.

Friend: But that's not... fair!

Director: What can I say?

Friend: But if you're predestined, one way or the other, isn't that a passive way to be? I mean, what choice do you have?

Director: We can choose to be what we are.

Friend: So the passive have to accept passivity?

Director: Sometimes the truth is ugly, yes. But really, Friend, we're just speculating here.

Friend: Which is to say we're not dealing in truth?

Director: We're trying to look the truth in the eye.

Friend: And when we do?

Director: We try not to blink.

18

Friend: Okay, but isn't the passive's acceptance of passivity an active thing? To accept is a verb.

Director: You have a point. So maybe they don't accept. Maybe they are what they are without knowing it themselves.

Friend: And the active know what they are themselves?

Director: Not always, no.

Friend: They mistake themselves for the passive?

Director: Sometimes, yes.

Friend: I don't know if I can believe any of this.

Director: Why not?

Friend: We're all born free, which is to say we're all born active.

Director: And?

Friend: Some of us sink into the passive.

Director: Is that a moral failure?

Friend: I'd say it is, yes.

Director: The active is moral and the passive is immoral?

Friend: Sure.

Director: But in the immoral, the person is at fault.

Friend: Of course.

Director: And if you're born passive, it's really not your fault.

Friend: That's the thing. That's why no one can be born passive.

Director: Because we really must have fault?

Friend: Yes.

Director: Fault for failing to be active.

Friend: Fault for being passive, yes.

Director: Why is passivity a moral failing?

Friend: The moral is a 'should'. We all should be active. Otherwise, we do harm to ourselves and others.

Director: We shouldn't do harm.

Friend: No, we shouldn't.

Director: What if the active do harm to the passive?

Friend: How do they harm them?

Director: They attack their passive ideas.

Friend: I think that's fine. But it's really not harm.

Director: It would be harm if they attacked their active ideas?

Friend: If they did damage, yes.

Director: Why do you say 'if'?

Friend: Because I'm not sure it's possible to harm an active idea.

Director: Active ideas are invulnerable? Does that mean the soul, the active soul, is invulnerable, too?

Friend: I think it does.

Director: What a life. You can't be touched.

Friend: Oh, you can be touched—just not in your soul.

Director: They can take away your job?

Friend: You know full well they can.

Director: They can take away whatever external thing?

Friend: Anything at all.

Director: But your soul remains intact.

Friend: Yes.

Director: What do you have when you have your soul?

Friend: The most important thing in the world.

Director: More important than food, shelter, and clothes?

Friend: What are those things without an active soul?

Director: Necessities, with or without the soul.

Friend: The soul comes first, then those things.

Director: That's fine. But can we agree the soul needs certain things to thrive?

Friend: Yes, of course. But it needs more than shelter, food, and clothes.

Director: Yes. It needs friends.

Friend: True! Active friends. A passive friend isn't really a friend.

Director: What's the act in friendship?

Friend: Love.

Director: Ah, I think you speak truth. But tell me. Is there such a thing as passive love?

Friend: Passive love isn't love.

Director: The passive of a thing isn't the thing.

Friend: True.

Director: Passive hope isn't hope?

Friend: Not at all.

Director: What about passive fear?

Friend: Count on you to ask.

Director: Well?

Friend: Fear might be the exception.

Director: Why?

Friend: Because fear... is fear!

Director: Can we say true fear is grounded in truth, and false fear is grounded in lies?

Friend: Not only can we say it—we'd be speaking truth!

Director: But fear is still fear.

Friend: Yes. But now that we're speaking of grounding, we can say hope is hope. It's just that false hope is grounded in lies.

Director: And the grounding determines how the thing feels.

Friend: Ah! You have a point. Feel is the thing. And it's true with fear, as well. True fear is more intense.

Director: Maybe it is, maybe it's not.

Friend: How could it not be more intense?

Director: True fear is under control in our minds.

Friend: But why be afraid if it's under control?

Director: Because we're aware of how easy it is to slip.

Friend: I'll have to think about that. But is your point that true fear is active?

Director: We're actively aware of just what's at stake.

Friend: At stake, interesting. We're afraid we'll lose something?

Director: The greatest thing we can.

Friend: Our soul.

19

Director: So true fear involves the soul.

Friend: Yes.

Director: And all other fears are false.

Friend: Well, I'm not so sure about that. We're afraid a mugger might kill us. That's a real fear that has nothing to do with our soul.

Director: And we're afraid we'll lose all our money in a great crash?

Friend: Yes, we're afraid of that, too.

Director: Maybe our soul is involved in these fears.

Friend: How?

Director: The fear of violent death, what does it mean?

Friend: What do you mean 'what does it mean'? We... fear death!

Director: But not the death of our soul?

Friend: I see what you mean. No, we know our soul lives on.

Director: We know it?

Friend: We believe.

Director: So we don't know. And when we don't know what we'd like to think we know, we fear. Fair enough?

Friend: Yes, that's fair enough.

Director: Now what about money?

Friend: That has nothing to do with soul.

Director: Are you sure? You just mentioned belief. Maybe we believe in what money can do for us?

Friend: We know what money can do for us.

Director: We know some things, yes. Money can buy an extravagant house. But we don't know if we'll be happy in that house.

Friend: True.

Director: So we believe in money and what it can do. Or, I should say, many believe in money and what it can do. And belief is of the soul. If we believe money does us good, we fear its loss.

Friend: But money does do us good. Food, clothing, shelter. These things are good. To do without them is bad.

Director: I agree. So the fear to lose them is true?

Friend: As true as true can be.

Director: And what about the extravagant house?

Friend: That's different.

Director: Because it's not necessary?

Friend: Yes.

Director: The necessary is true?

Friend: The necessary is true.

Director: We fear the loss of the necessary. Friends are necessary, aren't they?

Friend: I couldn't agree more.

Director: Fearing the loss of friends is true. But there's a problem here.

Friend: What problem?

Director: Sometimes we have to say difficult truths to friends, truths that might cause a break.

Friend: A true friendship won't break over that.

Director: That's where I'm not sure. Which is more important? The truth or the friend?

Friend: They're equally important.

Director: But if we had to choose?

Friend: You want me to say the truth.

Director: I do. I want you to say which is truly more important.

Friend: No, I mean you want me to answer that the truth is more important.

Director: No, I want you to speak the truth.

Friend: The friendship must be based on truth.

Director: Therefore?

Friend: Truth is more important here.

Director: Because without the truth, the friendship is false?

Friend: Yes.

Director: So it's an act of friendship to speak the difficult truth.

Friend: It is.

Director: And that's an active thing?

Friend: As active as can be.

20

Director: What's the passive thing here?

Friend: To hold the truth back.

Director: 'To hold' is an active verb.

Friend: So is 'to stick' your head in the sand.

Director: But when you hold, you hold the truth.

Friend: The truth must be shared among friends. You can hold and share at once. But holding back? That's a cowardly thing.

Director: Is cowardice always passive?

Friend: Of course it is. And all passivity is cowardly.

Director: Is all courage active?

Friend: Yes, no doubt.

Director: Is there a true courage and a false courage?

Friend: Sure. Foolhardiness is false.

Director: Is there a true passivity and a false passivity?

Friend: This gets back to your resignation. I thought it was passive of you, but you've given me reason to think otherwise. So, yes, there is seeming passivity, which is false; and then there's the passive which is true.

Director: And the truly passive is bad.

Friend: Bad as bad can be.

Director: Does that make the seeming passive good?

Friend: Of course not.

Director: Why not?

Friend: Everything to do with passivity is bad.

Director: Are we sure that's not just a bias of our times?

Friend: What! How can you even think that?

Director: I can think many things. My mind is active. And who knows? Maybe there really is a passive sight that's good.

Friend: No. 'To see' is active.

Director: Okay. But what's the opposite of sight?

Friend: Blindness.

Director: Is there an active verb for being blind?

Friend: I don't think there is. We just say, 'You are blind.'

Director: And 'are' is a form of 'to be'. Being. Passive or active? Tell me what you think.

Friend: If 'to be' is 'to thrive' it's active. If 'to be' is 'to rot' it's passive.

Director: The quality of being determines its state.

Friend: Yes.

Director: Can we go further? Can we say quality in general determines the state? And haven't we already been doing this when speaking of false and true?

Friend: I think you have a point. And we can say all good things are active, and all bad things are passive.

Director: Is truth good and falsehood bad?

Friend: Of course.

Director: Always?

Friend: What's with your 'always'? You're fishing around for some loophole here.

Director: I'm angling for the fish called truth.

Friend: And if that fish is no good?

Director: I'll make note of it, and throw it back in.

Friend: While we're at it, I'll note that the fish was passive; the fish was caught.

Director: Not if it allowed itself to be caught. Then it would only seem passive.

Friend: I suppose that's true, though you give too much credit to the fish.

Director: I'd only be inclined to give credit if there were something fishy in the catch.

Friend: Ha, ha.

Director: But let's get back to my loophole. You know the truth isn't always good. If you were hiding someone from the Nazis, and the Nazis came knocking on the door, would you tell them the truth?

Friend: No, of course not.

Director: Lying to them would be good?

Friend: Yes.

Director: So let's be clear. We've established that lying is sometimes good, and truth is sometimes bad.

Friend: And now we know what everyone knows.

Director: Yes, but everyone doesn't get too particular with these things. What makes the truth bad?

Friend: Bad consequences.

Director: And the false is good because of good consequences?

Friend: Yes.

Director: So we need to know what consequences are good and what consequences are bad.

Friend: That's easy enough to know.

Director: It's easy because to us Nazis are evil incarnate. Don't you think there are examples where it's a little more gray?

Friend: Yes, of course. But when it's gray we should stick with the truth.

Director: Why?

Friend: Because truth is good! The truth shines a light that leads us out of the fog.

Director: You make a good point.

Friend: Thank you. And I'll take it further. Lies add to the fog.

Director: So when we want daylight we stick with the truth; and when we want fog lies are the way.

Friend: Again, now we know what everyone knows.

Director: But each of these ways is active. We clear up the fog; we make more fog.

Friend: Agreed. And the passive is sitting around hoping the fog will thicken or clear.

21

Director: We must control the fog.

Friend: Masters of fog. Ha!

Director: You laugh. But do you agree?

Friend: I agree. Laughter isn't always a negative.

Director: But is it always active? What about a burst of uncontrollable laughter? Passive?

Friend: That's like saying thunder is passive.

Director: But thunder and laughs just happen. What's active there?

Friend: Maybe we should think of lightning. There's an active buildup of charge.

Director: And there's an active buildup to laughter? How?

Friend: You have to be prepared.

Director: You mean it's all in what you think?

Friend: Exactly!

Director: Certain thoughts predispose you to laugh?

Friend: At certain things, yes.

Director: But then is laughter something passive, something that just happens, the result of activity?

Friend: The active leading to the passive? Yes. But I don't like thinking of laughter as passive. It's such a wonderful thing.

Director: It truly is. Are you having trouble thinking of the passive as wonderful?

Friend: I am.

Director: Well, I can understand. We certainly don't like to think of passive as good. Especially not when it comes to very important things.

Friend: Things like what?

Director: Love.

Friend: True! Who wants a passive lover?

Director: Is it really love if one of the two is passive?

Friend: No, it's something else—something bad.

Director: Two active souls must meet?

Friend: Of course.

Director: And they're active because they think? Or are they active if they have an 'active lifestyle'?

Friend: Bah. That lifestyle talk is trash. Thinking is, and will always be, the truest active good.

Director: I'm impressed at the force of what you're saying. But what about the active heart? The truest active good?

Friend: Heart and mind are one—or should be one, that is. Don't you agree?

Director: I certainly do. I try to keep my two aligned.

Friend: Not aligned. One.

Director: Okay, but I'm wondering something. Is a heartbeat active or passive?

Friend: Count on you to ask me that. What do you think?

Director: Heartbeats are involuntary. That seems passive to me.

Friend: Then I take it so does falling in love?

Director: You have to be prepared for love.

Friend: I couldn't agree more.

Director: And now that I think of it, we can prepare ourselves for a healthy heart, through exercise and such. But we must admit, that doesn't always work.

Friend: We're not looking for 'always'. We're looking for the rule.

Director: And when we find the rule, what do we do with it?

Friend: Live by it! What else?

Director: How do we live by a rule?

Friend: We keep it always in mind.

Director: What if we forget?

Friend: What do you mean?

Director: What if we forget the rule?

Friend: How can we forget?

Director: I don't know. I forget certain things. Don't you?

Friend: You might as well forget your name!

Director: I've done that before.

Friend: Oh, you're being impossible.

Director: Maybe. But tell me this. Is forgetting active or passive?

Friend: Forgetting is passive—and bad.

Director: I think sometimes forgetting is good. Have you ever heard the saying 'forgive and forget'?

Friend: The saying is 'forgive but never forget'.

Director: Hmm. It seems we have dueling sayings here. I prefer to forgive and forget. That way my head, heart, soul, mind—whatever—is free.

Friend: But if someone truly wrongs you, how can you forget?

Director: If they change their ways? It's easy. I think of it no more. I actively stop the negative thoughts.

Friend: But people never really change their ways. That's why we must remember.

Director: Our sayings are based on one of the following views. People can change; people can't change.

Friend: It's not that they can't—it's that they don't.

Director: Ah, not 'always' again but 'the rule'.

Friend: Don't you agree that's the rule?

Director: I agree. True change is rare. And change is as active a thing as there is, I think.

Friend: What do you mean 'you think'?

Director: Haven't you heard change is the norm? 'The more things change, the more they stay the same.'

Friend: 'Things' change, Director. Things. People aren't things. People don't change.

Director: How are you so sure?

Friend: Oh, people change their opinions. People don't hold true. And that's the truth about them. But they rarely change their fundamental way.

Director: You want them to change in this.

Friend: For those we need to forgive? Of course I do!

Director: They'll change in this then change no more?

Friend: One last hurrah.

Director: And this change will be active?

Friend: Nothing more active.

Director: And then when they maintain, when they hold true? Active?

Friend: Holding fast is active. 'To hold' is a verb.

22

Director: Letting go is active. 'To release' is a verb.

Friend: We can go on and on like this.

Director: I'm sure we can. So what's the point?

Friend: To do something is active. To have it done to you is passive.

Director: But what if we provoke?

Friend: Provoking is active, but what you provoke is not. For instance, you provoked and were punched in the nose. Your nose did nothing active here.

Director: I see what you mean. So does provocation always have a passive result?

Friend: If the provocation is a success.

Director: Why do people provoke?

Friend: They want a response. Or they think they can get away with it.

Director: But if the latter, why bother? What comes of getting away with it?

Friend: Amusement?

Director: Maybe. And maybe they want to be punished.

Friend: Yes, I think that's true for some. And while we can punish ourselves very well, there's something special about being punished by another. There's a whole literature on this.

Director: I think certain people are attracted to passivity. To being punished by another, yes. But I think there's something more. There's something about the passive itself.

Friend: I think it has to do with laziness. You can't bother to lift a finger.

Director: But maybe someone else will?

Friend: Yes, and maybe snap yours off in the process. That risk is the thrill.

Director: So we have active thrill seekers, and passive thrill seekers. But let's bring this all home. The active are those who think. And the passive?

Friend: Are those who are thought?

Director: Interesting. They're captured in the thoughts of others?

Friend: Yes, I think that's true. They want to be captured that way. So they don't have to think.

Director: The awareness that comes of thought can be painful at first.

Friend: What's it like?

Director: Sometimes I think of it like a sunburn.

Friend: A sunburn's not so bad.

Director: No, but sun poisoning is.

Friend: Are you really saying there can be too much awareness?

Director: Too much all at once. These things take time, if we hope to mature.

Friend: So the passive are always unaware. They don't understand.

Director: And they're ignorant, too.

Friend: And if they're far enough gone, they'll never catch up.

Director: Catch up?

Friend: You know, to everyone else—to those who think.

Director: I'm not so sure about that.

Friend: Why?

Director: It's a mistake to think of these things as some sort of race. To think is good, even if only at the beginnings of thought. And I'll tell you this. Some who 'think' ignore these very beginnings that the once-passive come to know. The beginning is half of the whole. The wise stay closely in touch with their roots.

Friend: Okay, I see what you mean. So there's hope for the passive who come to think.

Director: There's hope for all who come to think.

Friend: How does someone decide to think? Is it always a choice?

Director: How does a child decide to walk? There's a moment of truth where it simply becomes possible, I think. Then the child takes that step. It might be the same with thought. Something within you embraces the possibility. It's as simple as that.

Friend: In other words, you don't really know if it's a choice.

Director: Right.

Friend: But once you've taken that first step, there's a choice. To think or not.

Director: I agree. Though I should mention that circumstances might overwhelm the tender shoot. And that's a shame.

23

Friend: The tender shoot of thought. How can we make it grow into a mighty oak?

Director: Wouldn't it be more of an evergreen? Either way, we nurture it like a little flame.

Friend: You switch metaphors and use 'nurture' just the same?

Director: What can I say? It's difficult to articulate these things.

Friend: So we want our thought to be a mighty blaze?

Director: A roaring fire, yes.

Friend: Then we need a proper hearth.

Director: Hmm. How do we make a fire strong?

Friend: We start with kindling to light the fuel.

Director: And that fuel is often chopped up trees.

Friend: Yes.

Director: What does firewood represent?

Friend: Dead and dried up ideas.

Director: And it's as simple as thinking about them and then they burn?

Friend: I suppose.

Director: The fire is active thought. But in order to think we must cut down trees.

Friend: I don't like this anymore.

Director: Why not?

Friend: We shouldn't cut down living ideas.

Director: What should we cut down?

Friend: Dead wood only.

Director: We can limit ourselves to that. And when we burn this wood, what do we have?

Friend: Light and heat and ash.

Director: Well, I think we should leave it there—because our metaphor is fundamentally flawed.

Friend: How so?

Director: Fire doesn't have to do anything in order to burn. We might even say it's passive.

Friend: The logs do all the work?

Director: No, the person who tends the fire.

Friend: Of course. And the fire is the mind.

Director: But we're up against it again. Don't we want to nourish the mind with living ideas?

Friend: We do. But unless we start a forest fire, we can't.

Director: Okay. So that seems to be as far as we can go with this.

Friend: I agree. But I'll add this. To start a forest fire is active. But once it's lit, there is no activity any more.

Director: Arson is active, yes. And criminal, too.

Friend: Can thought ever be criminal?

Director: We can have criminal thoughts, like thinking about stealing a car. But it's not illegal to think that thought.

Friend: What if we make certain thoughts illegal?

Director: That would be hard to enforce.

Friend: Maybe today. But with the technology of tomorrow?

Director: It might be possible.

Friend: I would want to burn that technology down.

Director: Or make sure it isn't put to bad use?

Friend: I would burn the bad uses down.

Director: Easier said than done. But to leave our metaphor behind, uses are often bad because they derive from a kind of deafness to reason. And when reason meets with the deaf...

Friend: ...reason isn't persuasive.

Director: Yes. It takes something more.

Friend: What more?

Director: It all depends.

Friend: Violence?

Director: Sometimes. There have been wars where reason is on a side against the deaf.

Friend: War makes me think of technology. Technology derives from reason, right?

Director: Not necessarily. There can be a certain momentum to these things that doesn't require active thought.

Friend: I've always believed that. But technology got its start from reason.

Director: I think that's true.

Friend: So technology and reason are closely related. My point is this. Because of this relation, only those who reason ought to be allowed to use technology.

Director: But, Friend, you can reason about one thing but not another. It happens all the time. Are you saying those who reason about pro football should be allowed to use technology?

Friend: No, those who reason about the technology itself.

Director: I see. But there was, and is, lots of technical reasoning about the atomic bomb. Should the scientists who reason about it be allowed to use it as they see fit?

Friend: Of course not. The reasoning must be about technology's use.

Director: You're assuming that to reason is always good. But there is dark reasoning, you know.

Friend: Tell me more about it.

Director: It's just reasoning you wouldn't allow to see the light of day. Secret reasoning. Think of it like this. When someone asks you why, and you merely say, 'I have my reasons,' you're keeping your reasons dark.

Friend: That's not so scary.

Director: No, it's not. But when do you keep your reasons dark?

Friend: When you know the other won't understand. When you know they'll have a bad reaction.

Director: How can we know these things?

Friend: We have to look for signs.

Director: How do we know what signs to look for?

Friend: Experience.

Director: What else?

Friend: Well, I suppose we can actively probe.

Director: Yes, I think that's best. Passive observance for signs might be useful, but it's not enough.

Friend: Why not?

Director: Because we might misinterpret the signs. When we probe we want to make sure there's no mistake.

Friend: So we observe and then we probe.

Director: We verify our observations.

Friend: But all of our observations?

Director: All of them.

Friend: Even the obvious ones?

Director: The obvious can be most treacherous.

Friend: Oh, now you're teasing.

Director: No, really. Verify it all. We want to be sure before we act.

Friend: But we'll seem ridiculous.

Director: Not once we've gathered all we need to know and execute our plan.

Friend: Plan?

Director: Do you really think we go into this without a plan?

Friend: I don't know. When do we formulate our plan?

Director: Once we've confirmed everything we think we know.

Friend: But if we have to confirm everything—everything—that will take... forever!

Director: Are you suggesting we never have a plan?

Friend: You're suggesting that, not me.

Director: What do you suggest?

Friend: I don't 'suggest' anything. I say we trust experience and act on that.

Director: But if your experience is with apples, and you're confronted with an orange....

Friend: I know that both are fruits and round. Beyond that, I couldn't say. But I can say much about fruit.

Director: What can you say?

Friend: Fruits go from unripe, to ripe, to overripe, to rot. That's important to know, don't you think?

Director: Yes, I do. You have a point. So what's your plan?

Friend: To eat the fruit before it rots.

Director: And a fine plan it is. Eating is an active thing. But rotting? That's emphatically passive. But then so is growing ripe.

Friend: How do you know? You're not a fruit. Maybe fruits have to work to grow ripe.

Director: A fair point. I guess I'd have to probe to find out. But let's forget about fruit.

Friend: Why? I think it's a very good metaphor.

Director: Yes, but fruits don't talk.

Friend: Your probing is all through talk, isn't it?

Director: Of course. Words are the window to the soul.

Friend: I thought it was the eyes.

Director: Certain words can light or dim the eyes.

Friend: That's how you know the words' effect?

Director: Yes.

Friend: What if your words have no effect at all?

Director: I'm probably talking with someone of little thought.

Friend: Maybe you just don't know the magic words.

Director: The words aren't magic. They're proven in success.

Friend: Success with apples doesn't mean you'll have success with pears.

Director: Humans aren't fruits. Humans are humans. And my words will have an effect on them.

Friend: You say that with such confidence.

Director: That's because I have a plan.

24

Friend: Tell me the plan.

Director: The plan is to encourage thought.

Friend: And what good will thought do?

Director: I don't know.

Friend: What do you mean, 'I don't know'?

Director: I don't know the particular good it will do, but I know it will do good—provided it isn't stifled and aborted halfway through.

Friend: We have to think things all the way through.

Director: Yes, we work out our problems this way.

Friend: But there are problems that can't be worked out through thought.

Director: Thinking will help us know this, and will help us know what to do.

Friend: You're a firm believer in thought.

Director: I don't believe; I know. I know the value of thought.

Friend: How are you so sure?

Director: From personal experience combined with experiments with others.

Friend: Experiments? What are you, some kind of thought scientist?

Director: Thought scientist. I think that fits, yes.

Friend: Tell me about these experiments.

Director: I work with the sick.

Friend: Mentally sick? As in mentally ill?

Director: Right, but not in the clinical sense.

Friend: What do you do with them?

Director: We discuss the sickness. But not in so many words.

Friend: Why not?

Director: If the sickness knew what we were up to, it would resist.

Friend: So it's an active sickness?

Director: No, it's the opposite of active. It resists thought.

Friend: Then what do you do?

Director: We set a trap. We think in almost a complete circle around the sickness.

Friend: Why not a complete circle?

Director: Because we want to leave an opening through which we'll drive the sickness out.

Friend: And when you drive it out you close the circle up?

Director: Yes, we close it up.

Friend: How many of the sick have you cured?

Director: Including myself? One.

Friend: What! Only yourself?

Director: We all must cure ourselves. Others can help us with our circle, but we must do the rest.

Friend: Why do you downplay your role?

Director: I don't.

Friend: Of course you do. You've cured more than one. And you did more than help with the circle. I think you helped drive the sickness out.

Director: I can suggest how it can be done. But it really is up to the other.

Friend: I bet you love to make that suggestion.

Director: I admit I like to stir the sickness up when it's time. But, really, then then other must drive it out. There's nothing here I can do.

Friend: And then they have to close the circle up?

Director: Positively. That's the one thing they must do completely alone.

Friend: I think I can see why. It's like setting a password that you and only you know. So then that's it?

Director: That's it—unless you have to do it all over again.

Friend: Why would you have to do that?

Director: Because you opened the circle to the sickness again. But that's enough about sickness. Let's talk about health.

Friend: Let me guess. Health is to think.

Director: Yes, and certain people resist their own health.

Friend: Is philosophy inherently healthy?

Director: Can you be sick and philosophize? I think the answer is yes. But in philosophizing you grow healthier than you were. But some think philosophy is a trick.

Friend: What kind of trick?

Director: Let me give an example. A philosopher once attempted to persuade a great tyrant to take up philosophy. The tyrant was torn. He wanted to be associated with philosophy. But he was afraid.

Friend: Why was he afraid?

Director: He thought the philosopher was trying to distract him, to cause him not to pay attention to his tyranny. And while not paying attention, he would be overthrown by the philosopher's friends.

Friend: Was that the philosopher's plan?

Director: He denied it.

Friend: Would the philosopher lie about this?

Director: Was he capable of lying? Yes. Did he? I don't know.

Friend: So you think philosophy can really be a trick?

Director: Not true philosophy. But 'philosophy'? Yes.

Friend: Why not true philosophy?

Director: Because thinking is to the tyrant's advantage.

Friend: Then why don't all tyrants think?

Director: Because tyrants attract 'philosophers'. And so when a real philosopher comes along they're wary.

Friend: But they don't need philosophy in order to think.

Director: That's true. But sometimes a word from a friend can go a long way.

Friend: So you're saying philosophers are the friends of tyrants?

Director: Philosophers can help tyrants become less bad. But for reasons which shouldn't surprise, the odds against this are long.

25

Friend: Surprise me. Why are the odds so long?

Director: Because the temptation to be passive in rule is strong.

Friend: What does it mean to be passive in rule?

Director: What it always means—not to think. But with those 'successful' in rule a certain reliance on luck creeps in.

Friend: Luck? You mean destiny.

Director: Yes. And part of this has to do with knowledge.

Friend: How so?

Director: From their vantage on high, rulers can see configurations and know what will come of them. So they sit back and let it all happen without giving it a thought.

Friend: Assuming what will happen is good, or at least 'good' for them.

Director: Yes, and you're right to qualify 'good'. Can you imagine someone seeing the bad and letting it happen?

Friend: Of course I can. The cowardly and lazy do this all the time.

Director: Are the cowardly always lazy and the lazy cowardly?

Friend: I think you can be lazy but not be a coward. And I think you can be a coward but not be lazy. But when the two go together....

Director: The worst of the worst?

Friend: Exactly.

Director: If you're cowardly-lazy, can you change?

Friend: I suppose it's possible. But I think it's rare.

Director: What could get you to step up and stop the bad thing you know is coming?

Friend: I'm not sure there is anything. What do you think?

Director: Self-interest.

Friend: Yes, but the cowardly-lazy don't know how to act in their self-interest. It takes something more.

Director: Fear.

Friend: Ah, a great motivator! Fear that they can't just sit back and watch. Fear that they're in the same boat as everyone else! That might do the trick. And if they're not afraid—we make them afraid!

Director: We shock them out of their passivity.

Friend: Yes!

Director: But what if to them, nothing's shocking?

Friend: That's the hardest case of all.

Director: What happens if there's a generation of these unshockables?

Friend: The nation is doomed.

Director: And if we see this, if we know this is what's happening?

Friend: We can be as active and brave as we like, but it won't matter.

Director: We fiddle while the nation burns?

Friend: Of course not. We pave the way to the new nation, the nation that will arise from the old.

Director: Will a virtuous nation always arise from the corrupt?

Friend: Not as a matter of necessity. We have to help bring this about.

Director: How?

Friend: By serving as examples to be emulated.

Director: We fly in the face of our corrupt nation?

Friend: We have to. Don't you think?

Director: I'm inclined to agree. And the more awful the backdrop the greater relief in which we'll stand?

Friend: That's exactly it. We have our chance to shine, thanks—to the decline.

Director: Let's be clear about something. Are we saying passivity is corruption?

Friend: That's what we're saying.

Director: And activity is virtue.

Friend: Yes, assuming the activity is good.

Director: But do we have to say, 'Assuming the passivity is bad'? Or are we saying all passivity is bad?

Friend: All passivity is bad.

Director: Will we try to win converts?

Friend: Among whom? The passive? Good luck with that. Our best chance is with the neutral.

Director: Neutral? Hold on. If you're neutral here aren't you passive? Or are you sometimes active, sometimes passive?

Friend: Sometimes this, sometimes that. But we want you to be always 'this'.

Director: And what's the advantage to them in being this?

Friend: They, too, can shine as examples.

Director: In other words, the reward is fame.

Friend: Yes.

Director: Sounds like a fair enough trade. Courage and activity to win yourself a name. How many will make the trade?

Friend: Not that many.

Director: How do you know?

Friend: In every corrupt nation, there have only been a handful who have stood out through virtue.

Director: Do you think it's by some sort of necessity?

Friend: There may be a hidden law here that we can't understand.

Director: Is it that to many, fame seems good—but they don't think it's worth the effort? Or does fame seem not so good to them?

Friend: I think there are two types of people, each with one of those views.

Director: Are there other views we should consider?

Friend: Well, I think there are those who think fame is bad.

Director: Okay. And then there's our view.

Friend: We have a view?

Director: Don't we? We think fame is good and worth striving for courageously. Or can we strive in a cowardly fashion?

Friend: Why would you even ask that?

Director: Because I want to know. Can we?

Friend: What would cowardly striving look like?

Director: You strive when the weather is fair, and hide when the weather is foul.

Friend: That won't win you fame. You have to strive in the foul. That's what will impress later generations.

Director: What if you're a coward your whole life and then at the end you have one courageous act. Fame?

Friend: That somehow doesn't seem fair.

Director: Do you admit this has happened?

Friend: I'm afraid it has.

Director: But doesn't that give you hope?

Friend: What are you saying? I'm a coward?

Director: No! Hope that all's well that ends well.

Friend: Tell me, Director. What if your whole life you're brave, and then right at the end—cowardice. Does it ruin your whole life?

Director: You're saying we have to constantly train for the end?

Friend: Of course we do. Actively train, train to be active and brave.

Director: Yes, though I suspect we more often than not train ourselves to be passive and cowardly—for not such a very good end.

26

Friend: So where does this leave us?

Director: It leaves me wondering about something we said. Fear as a motivator.

Friend: What are you wondering?

Director: Whether it's the exact opposite. Haven't you heard of being paralyzed by fear?

Friend: I have.

Director: Well, fear might not motivate—it might make things worse. And maybe that's the thing with the passive. They've been paralyzed, stunned into inactivity.

Friend: How can we help?

Director: We can remove them from the situation causing the fear and let them build up their nerve.

Friend: Nerve. True activity takes nerve. The passive lack nerve. I think it's true.

Director: Yes, but there may be exceptions.

Friend: Name one.

Director: You passively stand in front of an oncoming train, trusting that the driver will stop—or not. That takes nerve, don't you think?

Friend: You have a point. What about the active? And let's talk about thinking.

Director: Does it always take nerve to think? Not when there's nothing at stake.

Friend: But then is it really thought?

Director: An excellent question. What do you think?

Friend: Thought has to be about something. That 'something' is always at stake.

Director: What's the nature of being-at-stake?

Friend: Well, what's the 'something'?

Director: A belief.

Friend: Your belief might change because of your thought.

Director: Yes, but some are afraid of thought. What do you think that means?

Friend: It's evidence that you're a coward.

Director: But if something very real is at stake, shouldn't we be afraid but face up to our fear?

Friend: I suppose that's the definition of courage. So, yes, true thought is scary because something important is at stake. But the brave, the active, think nonetheless.

Director: Now let's ask the hard question. Is thought possible if you don't believe?

Friend: How can it be? What would you think about? No, there's no such thing as no belief. We believe all sorts of things. For instance, I believe when the light turns green it's safe to go.

Director: I always look both ways before I go. Sometimes drivers run the red light.

Friend: Well, yes. But you know what I mean. I believe the bridge won't fall down as I cross. And so on.

Director: I take your point. But do we spend any time thinking about the bridge?

Friend: No, but we pay others to do so for us.

Director: To think for us? What if this happens with more than bridges and the like?

Friend: You know it does.

Director: It happens with important things?

Friend: Sure, all the time.

Director: In an age of religion, people let others think for them about god?

Friend: Of course. Many do.

Director: And in an age of empire, people let others think for them about the imperium?

Friend: All the time. But not everyone does, Director. Some people think.

Director: And after they think, they act, so to speak?

Friend: Yes, they reaffirm or change their belief. And then sometimes they 'act' in the generally accepted sense.

Director: But if you change your belief don't you have to act in the generally accepted sense? Aren't you compelled?

Friend: You have a point. Beliefs cause actions.

Director: Holding the belief causes the action.

Friend: Right. If you let go, no action.

Director: The internal action, holding, causes the external action, whatever that might be.

Friend: Exactly.

Director: Can the holding cause other things?

Friend: Like what?

Director: Emotions.

Friend: Of course.

Director: What about anger?

Friend: If you hold a belief, and you see that someone you expect to hold that same belief doesn't, you might get angry at them.

Director: But why anger? Why not sadness?

Friend: Oh, there can be anger and sadness at once. The sadness just isn't noticeable because anger is so loud.

Director: Can the anger be defensive, protective?

Friend: That's a good insight. Yes, we cling to anger so we don't feel lost, hopeless.

Director: Hopeless because someone doesn't believe what we believe?

Friend: Certainly. Why, you don't think that's true?

Director: Anger prevents us from thinking. Anger is passive. So is hopelessness. No? If we're hurt that someone doesn't believe what we believe, we need to think, to check that belief.

Friend: And check the other's belief, too.

Director: Yes, check all the beliefs in play. Chances are good there's a problem with one or more of them here.

Friend: But something doesn't sit right. Is anger really passive? Doesn't holding our anger cause us to act on that anger?

Director: Prolonging our anger? Nurturing our anger? I still say that's passive. It puts off thinking. And if it makes us 'act', that action is without thought.

Friend: I think that's true. But I think there's something more, something I know from my own experience. We might think, arrive at a conclusion we don't like, then become angry as a reflexive means of rejecting that conclusion. But that's not to the point. What I want to know is whether any act without thinking is just an 'act'?

Director: Of course. Why, does that surprise you?

Friend: I guess it doesn't. But then so many acts are 'acts'. Again, I think there's something more.

Director: Oh?

Friend: A human who acts without thinking is just a 'human'.

Director: Shh! Someone might hear!

Friend: Stop teasing. I think you know very well what I mean.

Director: I do. But don't we all act without thinking at times?

Friend: We do. But some make it a habit.

Director: True. So, you're inclined to define humans as the thinking creature.

Friend: I am. Why, how would you define them?

Director: I'm with you. But maybe animals think, and think better, more clearly, than us.

Friend: I think things are very simple for animals.

Director: Maybe they should be with us, too.

Friend: True. So how would you simplify things?

27

Director: Do you want me to say I'd simplify our thought?

Friend: Isn't that the way?

Director: But today our thought is mostly simple.

Friend: So what should we do? Make our thought complex? Anything too complex is likely wrong.

Director: That might be true about ideas. But circumstances are often complex.

Friend: And when they are we need to go to the heart of the matter.

Director: The heart will always tell?

Friend: No matter how complex our lives might be, the heart will always tell.

Director: Are we talking about love?

Friend: We're talking about anything, including love.

Director: Love is simple.

Friend: But it can make things complex.

Director: How?

Friend: When we're afraid to admit the love.

Director: Or when the love makes us compromise our thought? Cloud our thought?

Friend: It's not love that clouds our thought. It's thought that clouds our love—bad thought.

Director: Good thinking keeps our skies clear—in or out of love.

Friend: Yes, and that only goes to show something very important. We must rely on ourselves if we want to see the blue.

Director: Relying on others clouds the sky?

Friend: Of course it does! Relying on others is passive. Relying on yourself is active.

Director: Why do you think people rely on others?

Friend: They're lazy, afraid—who knows?

Director: And what makes someone rely on themselves?

Friend: Pride.

Director: Ah. Pride. Can the passive feel pride?

Friend: I don't think they can.

Director: And the active?

Friend: Definitely.

Director: Passivity is the lack of thought? We're still saying that?

Friend: We are. And there's nothing to be proud of in not thinking.

Director: But maybe there's pride in getting others to do the thinking for you?

Friend: That's a sick sort of pride.

Director: Why?

Friend: It just... is!

Director: But don't you have to get others to do the thinking? Don't you have to spur them on? Isn't prodding a sort of action?

Friend: You're talking about an effort of one to get a return of ten.

Director: A good investment.

Friend: No! And I know you don't believe it.

Director: How do you know?

Friend: Because you're always thinking.

Director: But I spur others to think.

Friend: True, but you don't rely on their thought.

Director: Oh, but I do! I learn so much from them.

Friend: Learning and reliance are two different things.

Director: What's the difference?

Friend: When you learn you spur yourself. When you rely there's no self-spurring at all.

Director: What does the spurring?

Friend: What do you mean?

Director: I mean, what's the active part of us that spurs?

Friend: Why does it matter? What do you think it is?

Director: Ambition.

Friend: I don't know.

Director: Why not?

Friend: The passive can have ambitions.

Director: But if they're passive aren't those ambitions delusional?

Friend: Not if they have the ambition to be a puppet master pulling all of the strings.

Director: Can't you be an active puller of strings? Don't you have to give thought to which strings to pull?

Friend: We might as well say spiders are active. They create their web then actively wait on the flies.

Director: Spiders are patient. But if they're too patient they starve.

Friend: It's all in choosing the site for the web.

Director: They need knowledge of how to choose. How do they gain their knowledge?

Friend: Instinct.

Director: They don't learn by trial and error?

Friend: Oh, they might. But animals have instincts. Their knowledge is innate.

Director: Do humans have innate knowledge?

Friend: I think they do.

Director: How do we get at it?

Friend: We have to listen.

Director: Passively listen?

Friend: No, actively listen.

Director: What does that mean?

Friend: We have to act on what we hear.

Director: Oh. I thought it meant we have to question what we hear, then engage in a dialogue with ourselves.

Friend: Of course that's what you thought. Sometimes you just have to take things on trust, Director.

Director: And if you're wrong you can always go back and question. But maybe by then it's too late.

Friend: People who question their instincts end up in a muddle.

Director: Probably because the questioning wasn't very good.

Friend: What makes for good questioning here?

Director: Thoroughness. You can't just take one line of questioning. That will get you into a muddle. You have to take them all.

Friend: And when you have?

Director: You clear up anything that might be getting in the way of the truth.

Friend: The truth about the instinct.

Director: Yes.

Friend: Are you saying sometimes instincts are wrong? People don't believe that, you know.

Director: No, I know. Most people believe instincts are always right. Just as they believe first impressions are telling.

Friend: And they are.

Director: They can be, provided the person making the impression is acting in character, and the person observing isn't distracted by something else.

Friend: But we always act in character. That's why we call it character.

Director: There are special times when we don't act in character. And that can be more revealing than when we do.

Friend: What's such a special time?

Director: If we're normally passive, it's when we're active. If we're normally active, it's when we're passive. That reveals much.

Friend: So what do you recommend? We should goad people out of character?

Director: 'Goad' makes it sound like such a negative thing. 'Encourage' sounds better.

Friend: But you make it sound too positive. You make it sound like we're all too timid to step out of character from time to time.

Director: And most of us are.

Friend: And what do we get when we step out of character?

Director: An outside look in. Don't you think we can learn a lot from that? Won't that make us think?

Friend: Alright, you have a fair point. So how do you encourage this?

Director: We have a discussion about everyday things, and then, when the other says something curious, I question it gently.

Friend: And if they don't say anything curious?

Director: I have no business here.

Friend: That's it? You just move on to someone else?

Director: More or less? Yes.

Friend: So you're saying only certain people can step out of character?

Director: Of course. Some people are frozen solid within their character as though trapped in a block of ice.

Friend: But isn't that good? Not to be frozen, but to be firm in character?

Director: Firm is good. But being able to evaluate yourself makes firm better. Some of the 'firm' are passive. They are what they are purely through force of habit. Habit isn't active. Habit is passive. And habit kills the heart.

28

Friend: So we should have no habits?

Director: Things we do unthinkingly? What do you think?

Friend: 'It's the thought that counts.'

Director: Yes, though that saying suggests the deed wasn't what it should have been. And it suggests the thought wasn't what it should have been, either.

Friend: Good thoughts lead to good deeds.

Director: Right.

Friend: What's a good thought?

Director: A true thought.

Friend: What's a true thought?

Director: One that squares with the world.

Friend: What if the world is bad? Do bad thoughts square with a bad world?

Director: If so, does that mean good thoughts are out of step with that world?

Friend: Absolutely.

Director: I don't know, Friend. But let's say it's as you say. How does someone with good thoughts interact with a bad world?

Friend: He or she resists—actively resists.

Director: In order to protect the thoughts?

Friend: I never thought of it that way. But I'd say yes, though there's more than that to protect.

Director: Can you protect others with your good thoughts?

Friend: You certainly can, provided the thoughts are backed by deeds.

Director: But good thoughts are out of step?

Friend: Oh, I know you want to object. So I'll say this. Good thoughts are true. They describe the world well. But they're not one with it when it's bad.

Director: Does that mean good thoughts are at a remove?

Friend: Precisely.

Director: Hmm. That's starting to sound passive to me. The passive are always removed. Maybe we need to engage.

Friend: Engage this bad world? If we do, we engage to help our friends. Help save them from the world.

Director: And bring them to a world of our own?

Friend: Just so. And what's more active than creating your own world peopled with your friends?

Director: But where will we find the space in which to create this world? The 'world' is already taken.

Friend: We must fight for space, take it away from part of the world.

Director: The weaker part or the stronger part?

Friend: The weaker part is easier, don't you think?

Director: Yes, but then the stronger part might attack after we're somewhat weakened from our fight.

Friend: So what are you saying? It's best to fight the stronger part first?

Director: Fight them when we're fresh, yes. But let's recall what we're talking about. We mean to challenge them in thought.

Friend: Then we take on their strongest thinker first. But wait. That means that person is active.

Director: Yes?

Friend: Why would we fight the active?

Director: We seem to be forgetting ourselves. This person won't be active. They'll be 'active'.

Friend: Of course. And active always defeats 'active'.

Director: Well....

Friend: Well what?

Director: The 'active' usually fight thought by other means.

Friend: Violent means?

Director: Sometimes, yes—both physical and otherwise.

Friend: What's the otherwise?

Director: They do violence to thought.

Friend: You mean they lie.

Director: And use every dirty trick there is in support of their lies.

Friend: That's true. So we have to fight fire with fire!

Director: Aren't you worried we'll forget what we're about in using such means?

Friend: No, we won't forget. We'll always remind each other.

Director: But the tricks you're talking about are tricks of the passive. Do we become passive in order for activity to prevail?

Friend: We merely pretend we're passive.

Director: But this is a long term fight. If we always pretend, or pretend long enough, isn't there a risk we'll become what we pretend?

Friend: You worry too much. Remember. We're actively pretending we're passive. That activity keeps us alive.

Director: Maybe. But how many of the passive pretend they're only pretending to be passive for a limited time?

Friend: I don't think they're that aware.

Director: People are more aware than we think. That's why they get upset with discussions like this. If they weren't aware, why would they?

Friend: They know they're passive?

Director: Of course they do. But the worst of them think they're wise.

Friend: And we show them what their wisdom is worth—nothing.

Director: Or worse.

Friend: So how do we carve out a world for the active?

Director: Thinking necessitates carving out a world of your own.

Friend: Your own? We don't join together?

Director: Not in the world-creating activity, no.

Friend: But when we've created our worlds?

Director: We admire one another, my friend.

29

Friend: No, that's not enough. We need to be together. Who can live by having a world and admiring the worlds of others? You're isolated that way.

Director: Then what do you propose?

Friend: Admire, but live together. That's what friends do.

Director: And if my world differs from yours?

Friend: We find the common ground and make allowances for the rest. Again, that's what friends do.

Director: Finding is active. It takes thought.

Friend: Of course it does.

Director: But what about making allowances? Active?

Friend: When you make an allowance you have to find a way to live with that allowance. Active.

Director: Finding. Maybe that's what all thought is—a sort of search.

Friend: That sounds right to me. We search for the truth. We search for a way.

Director: And maybe the truth helps us find a way.

Friend: I wouldn't say 'maybe'. I'd say it certainly does.

Director: Truth and a way. What more does anyone need?

Friend: Yes, but sometimes the times get dark.

Director: We can't see our way.

Friend: Right. We need light.

Director: The light of truth?

Friend: That's not enough.

Director: Then what do we need?

Friend: The light of love.

Director: They say love will find a way.

Friend: And they're right! It's just that sometimes it takes a while.

Director: Like a couple of hours?

Friend: Ha! Like a couple of years!

Director: Then maybe love's not so good at finding the way. It might take something more.

Friend: Like what?

Director: I don't know. But wait! I do know! Philosophy.

Friend: Of course that's what you'd say. Philosophy finds a way. Always?

Director: Always.

Friend: But some philosophers spend decades trying to find a way.

Director: But they find little ways on the way to the big way. Tributaries to the larger flow.

Friend: Don't tell me philosophy is all about flow.

Director: I won't—because flow is passive.

Friend: But we all want flow. How can flow be bad?

Director: I'm not saying it's bad.

Friend: Then flow is the only passive good.

Director: Don't be so sure. But you know, achieving flow takes effort.

Friend: How so?

Director: You have to dredge the channel.

Friend: And what's the channel?

Director: Your heart and mind. That's where flow takes place. Don't you agree?

Friend: I agree. But what exactly are we dredging?

Director: Many things. Maudlin sentiments. Half-digested ideas. You name it.

Friend: And how do we dredge?

Director: We think.

30

Friend: I agree that thought can digest an idea. But take away a feeling?

Director: When we digest ideas our feelings often change. They become optimized for flow. When they're not, they're a drag.

Friend: So what are you saying? It's perfect thought for perfect flow?

Director: At risk of sounding facile, yes.

Friend: But my perfect flow will be different than your perfect flow.

Director: True.

Friend: So my perfect thought will be different than your perfect thought.

Director: Right.

Friend: But perfect should be perfect for all!

Director: Why?

Friend: Because!

Director: One great Because to everyone's Why?

Friend: Yes! That's what we desperately need.

Director: Can't you see how passive that is? Who is the keeper of The Because?

Friend: We all are.

Director: Sure. But in practice?

Friend: I don't know.

Director: You don't? Who has been the keeper of The Because? Historically.

Friend: Priests?

Director: Priests, in all their many forms and names. Tell me. Is it active or passive to receive the truth from them?

Friend: You're oversimplifying things.

Director: How so?

Friend: It's not like there's some magic litany that when known will reveal The Because.

Director: Really? Are you sure? I've come across a few in my day.

Friend: Yes, but did the priests want you to passively accept them? Or did they challenge you to think?

Director: I wouldn't say they challenged me to think. They challenged me to believe. That's what priests want, all priests—belief. Do you deny that?

Friend: Well, you may have a point.

Director: If a priest challenges you to think, which they often seem to do, they want you to conclude your thought in strengthened belief. That's what fools many would-be thinkers. 'How can it be bad if it makes me think?' But we need to have the courage to take our thought all the way.

Friend: For the sake of flow.

Director: Flow, sure. But that's just a promise. We have to take our thought all the way—come what may.

Friend: In other words, we have to believe in thought.

Director: No. There are signs along the way that tell us thought is good. If we don't see those signs, we can always stop. But I see the signs. And so I keep going.

Friend: But going where?

Director: Wherever my thought takes me. That's why my perfect thought differs from yours, or anyone else's. We each have our own journey in life. When we give that up, we're lost.

Friend: But we don't know where we're going!

Director: You want a Because to tell you where you're headed? I'd rather have so many smaller becauses along the way. And sometimes they're not so small.

Friend: Why can't there be active belief? True belief isn't passive. You have to work at your belief.

Director: Work to suppress your thoughts? Sorry, I couldn't resist.

Friend: There's such a thing as a bad thought, you know.

Director: Can you give an example?

Friend: Wishing harm on another.

Director: Wishes aren't thoughts.

Friend: How about this? Thinking someone is bad and deserves to come to harm.

Director: Maybe that person is bad and deserves to be punished. We'll never know unless we think.

Friend: Is there anything you wouldn't think about?

Director: Nothing.

Friend: But haven't you ever heard someone say, 'Don't even think it'?

Director: Of course I have. And I take that as an invitation to think.

Friend: Do you love to think?

Director: Yes. And I wish more people did.

Friend: But what if they think about you?

Director: They'd find some good and some bad. Why?

Friend: I don't want people to think about me.

Director: But you can't control that. What will you do? Stick your head in the sand? That would make someone like me think all the more.

Friend: But people won't have it.

Director: Have what?

Friend: Your thinking about them.

Director: But how will they know?

Friend: They can tell. A word let slip. A telling glance or smile. You can't help yourself here.

Director: Well, what's the good of thought if you can't even smile?

Friend: But your smile will infuriate some.

Director: That's the chance I take. Or do you think I should be more prudent?

Friend: I do! Why do you think they made you resign?

Director: One too many smiles?

Friend: Yes! They know what you think of them.

Director: And now I know what they think... of me.

31

Friend: It's better not to find out.

Director: I don't agree.

Friend: Why do you care what people think of you?

Director: Aren't you the one who cares?

Friend: Oh, this is all nonsense. Let's get back to active and passive. Do you actively care what people think of you?

Director: I comb my hair. I wear nice clothes. I'm very polite. I suppose I must actively care what people think.

Friend: Yes, yes. But that's just on the surface.

Director: What more is there?

Friend: The depths!

Director: I don't want to get into the depths with my colleagues.

Friend: Why not?

Director: Would you believe me if I told you it would get in the way of our work?

Friend: Not for a moment. I'm a colleague, and here we are in the depths.

Director: But you're not just a colleague. You're a friend.

Friend: And you care what I think?

Director: Of course.

Friend: On the surface or in the depths?

Director: Both.

Friend: And you only care about both with friends?

Director: In order to deal with the depths, friendship is required.

Friend: I've never heard that before. Can you say more?

Director: In every true friendship there is trust. If you want to probe the depths, that's what you need.

Friend: Why?

Director: Isn't it obvious?

Friend: But you can trust someone without being their friend.

Director: Friendship makes it better.

Friend: Okay. But what would you do if someone you didn't trust tried to probe your depths?

Director: What would you do?

Friend: Push them away.

Director: Or?

Friend: Or what?

Director: Lie?

Friend: What would you do?

Director: I would tell them the truth.

Friend: No! You can't trust them. Why tell them the truth?

Director: What can I possibly have to hide?

Friend: You're either lying to me now or else you're naive. And I don't think you're naive.

Director: Why would I lie about this?

Friend: Why won't you lie to them?

Director: Because then I'll never know what they think.

Friend: Of course you will! Just not what they think about you.

Director: But that's what I want to know.

Friend: I thought it wasn't all about you. I thought it was about ideas.

Director: And it is. But I want to know what idea they have of me.

Friend: That's a dangerous thing, Director.

Director: Why?

Friend: We live in a time of a war of ideas.

Director: Many times have been a time of a war of ideas.

Friend: And that doesn't matter. What matters is that we live in such a time now.

Director: How do you suggest I wage my war?

Friend: It's best not to fight.

Director: Really? Stick my head in the sand?

Friend: No. Just avoid confrontation when you can.

Director: And what will that get me?

Friend: Peace.

Director: And when I can't avoid confrontation?

Friend: Lie.

Director: Are you assuming the enemy is so strong we can't stand up and openly fight?

Friend: The enemy is very strong these days.

Director: Who is this enemy?

Friend: Don't you know? The passive, in all their might.

Director: These non-thinkers, do they want to know what I think?

Friend: Of course they do! They always do.

Director: Because?

Friend: Thought is bad.

Director: Why is it bad, to them?

Friend: Because they lie.

Director: To whom?

Friend: Themselves and everyone else.

Director: Why do they lie to themselves?

Friend: Because that's how they construct their personality.

Director: This sounds profound.

Friend: It's actually very simple. We live in a land where you can be whatever you want.

Director: We do?

Friend: In theory. Some act on that theory and create what they want with lies.

Director: Because it's easier to be in-lie than in-fact.

Friend: Right.

Director: That's easily understandable. And thinking exposes the lies.

Friend: That's why they hate thought.

Director: That, too, is easily understandable.

Friend: So now do you see?

Director: See the need to avoid their hate? Who wants to be hated? But if it comes down to snuffing out my thought—I won't, and never will.

Friend: No one's asking you to snuff out your thought. You just need to learn to hide it a bit.

Director: But isn't hiding your thought a sort of lie?

Friend: Yes, that's true.

Director: So we fight lies with lies.

Friend: That's only right.

Director: If only we were really fighting those lies. Hiding thought is no fight.

Friend: Well, that's true, too. How would you fight?

Director: I'd ask them questions about what they believe.

Friend: Because they believe their own lies.

Director: Yes. I'd expose the lies.

Friend: And that will get you nowhere!

Director: It's not about me getting somewhere. It's about getting them to reform.

Friend: I know you can't believe that. Nothing will reform these people, least of all you!

Director: Alright. I got a little carried away.

Friend: If you can't reform them, why expose them?

Director: So others can see them for what they are. Others who have a chance at being true.

Friend: You make it sound like falsehood rubs off.

Director: If the false are those you're taught to respect? Maybe it does.

32

Friend: I think you get something out of it, too. I think you enjoy exposing the false.

Director: I'd be lying if I told you otherwise.

Friend: There's something wrong about that.

Director: Something wrong about enjoying good work? What would you have me enjoy? Bad work?

Friend: You know what I mean.

Director: I really don't. Why shouldn't I enjoy something that will help others and myself?

Friend: How will it help you?

Director: I don't go into it thinking, 'Now I'll expose the false!' I go into it thinking, 'Maybe they know something I don't know.'

Friend: I don't believe you. What could you possibly learn?

Director: How to live my life.

Friend: From those you don't respect?

Director: You're assuming I only challenge those I don't respect. The truth is I don't much bother with them. I challenge the ones I respect. That's why I hope to learn.

Friend: But you end up proving them false?

Director: Sometimes, in certain things. And I'd hope they'd return the favor. The false is a temptation to us all. Friends should keep friends honest.

Friend: But what you're saying doesn't add up. You said you want to expose the false for others to see. Is that what friends do?

Director: I don't so much expose the friend as I expose the lie. But I do expose the lie to the friend.

Friend: In hopes they'll change?

Director: Yes.

Friend: I still don't buy it. I think you attack your enemies this way.

Director: My enemies attack me. I defend myself with truth. That often exposes their lies.

Friend: So unless attacked you don't expose the false except with friends?

Director: Correct.

Friend: So you passively wait to be attacked.

Director: There's not much waiting involved. An upright man always makes a tempting target.

Friend: But if you cringe?

Director: You're less likely to be attacked, though more likely to be abused.

Friend: That's our choice in life? To be attacked or abused?

Director: Or to get away from the false, all of the false, as often as we can.

Friend: And that's why you want to expose the false in yourself and your friends, so you can have a haven of truth?

Director: You put that very well.

Friend: What's false in me?

Director: Maybe what's false in me, too.

Friend: What can that be?

Director: The belief that passivity is always bad.

Friend: I thought we went over this.

Director: Yes, but I think we're forgetting one important thing. How we must endure when there's nothing to be done.

Friend: But how do we know there's nothing to be done?

Director: We explore all the possibilities, and we remain open to them even when we find there's nothing to be done.

Friend: But can't we say endurance is active?

Director: We can say it, but is it? Really? What do we do, actually do, when we endure?

Friend: We remain composed.

Director: We compose ourselves. We compose ourselves to remain passive. Our activity supports our passive stance. To me that sounds... passive.

Friend: Well, there's passive and then there's passive.

Director: Is there? Or are you saying that if you're going to give up you might as well strike a good pose?

Friend: Don't you ever endure?

Director: All the time.

Friend: You seem composed to me.

Director: There's a reason for that. I'm concentrating.

Friend: On what?

Director: The possibility that there might be something to be done.

Friend: You're always looking for that chance?

Director: Always.

Friend: Doesn't that get exhausting?

Director: Not as exhausting as it would be if I lost my composure. Have you ever done that?

Friend: Of course.

Director: Were you at peace?

Friend: Far from it. And it was exhausting.

Director: Then staying composed when you're passive makes good sense.

Friend: We should stay composed when we're active, too.

Director: Certainly. We should always stay composed.

Friend: Always? I thought philosophy shied away from 'always'.

Director: When should we lose our composure? Or rather, when should we let loose? When explosive behavior is our only way out of a bad situation. When we have no other choice. When staying composed would be the end.

Friend: I thought philosophers faced their end boldly.

Director: Yes, but that doesn't mean they sacrifice themselves.

Friend: Isn't that how philosophy was founded? Through a sacrifice?

Director: The religion of philosophy, yes.

Friend: And you're a devotee of that religion?

Director: Not at all.

33

Friend: But how can that be? You always talk about philosophy.

Director: There's philosophy and then there's philosophy.

Friend: And yours is philosophy with a capital P?

Director: No, it's the other way round.

Friend: Do you have to defend yourself from Philosophy with a capital P?

Director: Funny you should ask. That philosophy ignores me as a mere nuisance.

Friend: Do you attack it?

Director: I prod and probe. It gets annoyed. But by its own principles it won't attack me.

Friend: Do you want it to attack?

Director: If it did, that would expose a few lies.

Friend: So you keep on hoping it will. Look at you smile!

Director: I think of that sort of philosophy as a wayward cousin. I'm just looking for a moment of truth that might bring it back.

Friend: Have you ever had such a moment of truth?

Director: Once, yes. With a young philosopher.

Friend: What happened?

Director: He came over to philosophy with a lower case P.

Friend: And now you two philosophize together?

Director: Not at all. He went his separate way.

Friend: That's too bad.

Director: No, it's actually good. Philosophy in our sense stands a better chance when we fan out.

Friend: So if I became a philosopher you'd want me to leave?

Director: I would and I wouldn't. It's like when a child leaves home. You want it to go but you don't.

Friend: What does that make you? The father of philosophy?

Director: At best maybe a father of philosophy.

Friend: Well, I don't want to father any philosophical brats. And since I'm not going anywhere you'll just have to put up with me.

Director: And I will with true passivity.

Friend: Ha! You'll endure my presence?

Director: None of us is perfect. There are things about me you have to endure, just as there are things about you I have to endure.

Friend: Not 'have' to endure—'choose' to endure.

Director: Choose, yes. I like that better, too.

Friend: When we endure we learn. And learning isn't passive. I actively learn from you.

Director: I believe you. But I don't believe it's through what you endure. Learning is a pleasure. You don't have to endure the pleasant. Or don't you think learning is such?

Friend: Many would say learning is hard.

Director: Learning what you don't want to know is hard.

Friend: What do we want to know?

Director: It differs from person to person. And that's another passive thing. Want. We can't help what we want.

Friend: I thought you'd say we can change our thinking and thereby change what we want.

Director: We can think how to satisfy want, and when we do satisfy our want, that's what might change what we want.

Friend: So some people want philosophy and some people don't. You wouldn't say everyone really wants philosophy but just doesn't know it yet?

Director: This is a difficult question because it gets into the question of what a person is.

Friend: I should have known not to bring it up. Why does it get into that?

Director: A philosopher is a different kind of person than a non-philosopher. Do you agree?

Friend: People are people.

Director: But that's the thing. You either think there are different kinds of people or you don't. It all starts there. Do you really think all people are alike?

Friend: In one sense, yes. But of course there are differences.

Director: I'm inclined to think those differences are more important than the similarities. That's where I begin. How about you?

Friend: I never thought of it as an opening step before. Why do we have to decide?

Director: If you want to go somewhere you have to take the first step. So what's more important?

Friend: They're equally important. I guess I'm staying right here.

Director: Suit yourself. But some day you might have to choose.

Friend: And choice is active.

Director: Right. The passive fail to choose, in part because they want to have it both ways. They're paralyzed by their desire.

Friend: But you said we can't help what we want.

Director: And I said when we satisfy a desire our desires can change. That's why we have to choose. To free ourselves from conflicting desires. Or we can go on and satisfy neither.

Friend: What's the more active choice?

Director: The one that goes against the spirit of the age.

Friend: Does the spirit always come from the majority?

Director: No. One can have more spirit than ten.

Friend: So are we simply contrarian? We go against the spirit from wherever it might come?

Director: All I can say is we hold difference dear because it's in danger of being washed away.

Friend: Ha! Fat chance of that.

Director: Really? What's the most important difference?

Friend: What we've been talking about—activity versus passivity.

Director: Can't you see the possibility of thought, the active, being washed away?

Friend: Thought, like hope, will spring eternal.

Director: Will it? I'm not so sure. It's easy not to think. And if everyone you know isn't thinking....

Friend: Tell me this. Who thought the first thought? And was it an accident?

Director: Someone chose to fight the passive. It was no accident. But I don't think there was just one. Several chose to fight. And when they finally encountered one another...

Friend: What?

Director: ...there was recognition—and hope.

34

Friend: But how would they even know what the passive is if there was no thought? Do you know what I mean?

Director: The only way I can explain it is this. It's night, and all is dark. But then a thunderstorm rolls in. Suddenly a bolt of lightning illuminates the sky. That bolt is thought. And it's as clear as day.

Friend: And what's the active part in that?

Director: We can't get too particular. It's just a metaphor. And probably a poor one at that.

Friend: On the contrary. I think it's rather powerful.

Director: What seems the active part to you?

Friend: The thunder rolling in. The thunder comes from resistance, active resistance.

Director: Resistance to what?

Friend: Passive acceptance of all that is.

Director: The equation of 'is' with 'must be'?

Friend: Yes.

Director: Then thought is predicated on the notion of change, of the possibility of change?

Friend: It must be. Don't you think?

Director: I do think. But I wonder about all this change.

Friend: Here's the irony. We live in an age of constant change. But it's change within certain limits.

Director: Is it like being trapped in a washing machine that agitates us no end and keeps us locked within its drum?

Friend: Exactly! That's how it is. Can we think our way free?

Director: Again, it's just a metaphor. But can we escape the limits of our age? It's possible.

Friend: How do you know it's possible? Have you?

Director: How would I know if I had?

Friend: What do you mean?

Director: I mean, if you cross what you thought was a limit, and there are no terrible consequences, there was no limit. Do you see?

Friend: Yes, I see. The limit was in your thought. But I think we need certain limits in thought.

Director: Such as?

Friend: The limit that says you shouldn't kill those you hate.

Director: That's a good limit.

Friend: Yes, and there are many others like this.

Director: And combined they make up the limits of the age?

Friend: I think that's true.

Director: So if we want to go beyond the limits of the age....

Friend: We should kill?

Director: No, I'm not saying that. I'm saying we should think about the little limits and decide whether they're good or bad. That's how we start to go beyond.

Friend: What if we think they're all good?

Director: Then we're going nowhere but here. No beyond.

Friend: Why do you think one person wants to be here and another wants beyond?

Director: The former doesn't feel constrained. The latter does.

Friend: I feel constrained by this place. I want beyond.

Director: Can you identify a limit you might set aside?

Friend: I think that's a private thing.

Director: Alright. But don't let privacy be a limit for you.

Friend: Privacy is a freedom.

Director: Is it? Not always, I think. But on the whole? Yes.

Friend: So glad you agree. But why wouldn't it be a freedom?

Director: When it becomes musty and full of passivity. Sometimes it takes the light of friends to sanitize things.

Friend: That's the thing. Privacy we can control. Who we let in.

Director: And when we go out. There's freedom in stepping out.

Friend: Of course there is. I take the point. For some, stepping out amounts to crossing a boundary. And this is often good.

Director: When is it good?

Friend: When we feel an urgent need to share.

Director: But sometimes we have to hang fire.

Friend: Why?

Director: You need the right person in order to share.

Friend: Of course. You can't just share with anyone. Unless... you give hints, hints that only the right person will understand.

Director: I'm sure there's something to that. But I'd spend more time searching than hinting.

Friend: But hints can be the bait to bring your big fish in! What's the harm?

Director: I suppose there's no harm. But don't be too subtle or no one will understand.

Friend: What if I want someone subtle?

Director: I said don't be too subtle. Subtlety is fine. Excessive subtlety is the mark of the passive.

Friend: Why is it passive?

Director: Because no one will understand—and the passive like it that way. When someone understands you, you're compelled to act.

Friend: I'm not sure I understand why that is.

Director: You must confirm or deny the understanding.

Friend: Why would you deny?

Director: Let's say you have the habit of stealing pie from the refrigerator at work. Someone understands this about you, this weakness of yours. And they let you know. Do you confirm?

Friend: Well, that's an embarrassing situation. I probably wouldn't confirm.

Director: Can you imagine other things like this in life?

Friend: Of course. I take your point. But that means it's only bad things you don't confirm?

Director: Maybe you wouldn't confirm something good. Let's say you leave an envelope with money in it for the cleaning staff at work every so often. You don't want to be known. But someone says they know about and understand this weakness of yours. Do you confirm?

Friend: I want to be anonymous. So, no. But why do they say it's a weakness?

Director: Oh, I don't know. They're cynical probably.

Friend: Cynicism is passive. You don't have to think. You just assume everyone is motivated purely by self-interest.

Director: I think there's a passive component to it, yes. Any kind of -ism has a passive component. But there can also be activity. You might think about just what the self-interest is, in our example.

Friend: True. But it's thought within bounds. All -isms are thoughts within bounds. And the more you think within them, the deeper the rut you're in.

Director: Because it becomes a habit of mind.

Friend: Yes.

Director: Unbounded thought is pure activity.

Friend: I agree.

Director: And it generates further activity as we act in other ways to confirm and sustain our thought.

Friend: Of course.

Director: Confirming our thought is easily understandable. But how do we sustain our thought?

Friend: You should tell me.

Director: Alright. We have to arrange our lives in such a way that we lend support to thought.

Friend: How can we do that?

Director: For instance, you give up a job that makes you crazed for long hours and unable to think from exhaustion when you're done.

Friend: How else can we lend support to thought?

Director: You end a relationship that drains you emotionally, leaving you unable to think. But there are positives, too. You develop relationships that are conducive to thought. My relationship with you, for instance.

Friend: Yes, that makes sense. And there are jobs that are conducive to thought, I'm sure.

Director: Can you name such a job?

Friend: Sure. You might be a professor.

Director: Professors profess what they know.

Friend: And they're always learning new things. And their students might stimulate thought. You should be a professor!

Director: Ah, but there are some very big -isms that come along with the job. I'm not sure that's for me.

Friend: What -isms?

Director: They have to do with student expectations. They pay a lot of money, you know. But there's another more troubling thing. You don't get to choose your students.

Friend: So?

Director: There might not be much understanding in class.

Friend: You have to teach to their level.

Director: I don't have to—because I choose not to teach.

35

Friend: Start your own school.

Director: I already have.

Friend: What! When? Where?

Director: Many years ago. Right here.

Friend: But where are your students?

Director: They learned and then they moved on.

Friend: How long is your course of study?

Director: It varies. For some, a few months. For others, a couple of hours.

Friend: What can you learn in a couple of hours?

Director: You can have your thoughts confirmed. That goes a long way, you know. Thoughts you thought were yours alone. You learn they're not. This strengthens them. It proves you're not crazy after all.

Friend: But what if you, the teacher, are crazy? The crazy confirms the crazy!

Director: Don't you think that happens in universities every day?

Friend: No! I think it rarely happens. The problem with your method is that you have no colleagues, no administration to keep you in line. You might drift into crazy and no one would know.

Director: You underestimate my students. They know crazy very well, can see it right away. They very much keep me in line.

Friend: How do you know they know crazy very well?

Director: Because they flirt with it every day.

Friend: And you pull them back from the edge? How?

Director: Crazy happens when the otherwise active mind goes passive on certain things. I encourage them to think about those things. Think them through.

Friend: I think people can go crazy from thinking too much.

Director: Yes and no. If you think but don't think fully, comprehensively, you will cause a sort of misshape to your brain, mind, soul. If you're going to think, you need to think all the way.

Friend. All the way to what?

Director. To the end of your life. But that can be taken in two senses.

Friend. What do you mean?

Director. It can mean until the end of your life as in death. Or it can mean until you find the end, the purpose or goal of your life.

Friend. And then you stop thinking?

Director. No. Then you have to think your way back to the start and begin anew, this time with clear headed purpose.

Friend. You're making your whole life active.

Director. That's right.

Friend. That can be taken in two senses.

Director: Oh?

Friend: The first sense is 'that's correct'. The second sense is 'that's what right is'.

Director. Both senses are true. The right life is the active life. Yes.

Friend: What of the thinkers who merely contemplate the truth. That's not an active life, is it? That's not the right life.

Director: It depends. If contemplation spurs thought, then it's good, regardless of whether it's passive or active. But if nothing comes of it?

Friend: It can't be good.

Director: Yes, but it might be a harmless activity, a neutral activity, and therefore not bad.

Friend: Most people think that neither-good-nor-bad is bad.

Director: Perhaps most people haven't thought it through.

Friend: What's to think? Good is good. Bad is bad. And neither is neither.

Director: I think the problem is that people always want people to take a side. They want it all black and white.

Friend: Why do you think that is?

Director: It's easier that way, less active. Three things are harder to juggle than two.

Friend: And you're more active if you juggle a hundred?

Director: I wouldn't call trying the all-but-impossible active.

Friend: Why not?

Director: When efforts get too complex rational thought is no longer possible. We find ways to cheat. The cheating is passive.

Friend: But some can handle more complexity than others.

Director: That's true. But the temptation to cheat is strong when you operate near your limit. Better to juggle three and be sure. Besides, you'll be more easily understood by others this way.

Friend: I've noticed that when people want to obfuscate they grow increasingly complex in what they say.

Director: It's best to keep it clear and take it step by step; though some will think this shows a lack of understanding on your part, a lack of refinement, a lack of class.

Friend: Who cares? So long as the thought is clear, that's all.

36

Director: Tell me, Friend. Why do we want clear thought?

Friend: So we're sure we understand, and so we can communicate well with others.

Director: And that communication is active?

Friend: Yes, of course.

Director: Do you think passive communication is even possible?

Friend: How could it be?

Director: Well, I've puzzled over this a bit. What if you have one active communicator who explains things to a passive-minded person, who then in turn communicates this to a third active-minded party?

Friend: There will be transmittal errors.

Director: Yes, almost certainly. But what if enough of the message gets through so that it's intelligible to some degree?

Friend: Well, then it's communication to some degree. And it might be enough to prompt the active-minded recipient to think.

Director: Yes, that would be the hope. But there's so much room for misunderstanding. So the question is whether it's best not to communicate to the passive at all, even if it's the only means of communication open at a time, or to risk misunderstanding and proceed.

Friend: I think it's worth the risk.

Director: But the problem is you can't alienate the passive or they'll never pass your message on.

Friend: So you flatter them?

Director: No, but I don't go out of my way to turn them off. If I can stay on my way and communicate my thought and have it received in good will, I will. So where does that leave us?

Friend: We stay on our way and speak our minds, without giving undue offense.

Director: How do we know when offense is undue?

Friend: If it serves no purpose.

Director: Oh. I thought you were going to say something else.

Friend: What 'something else'?

Director: Undue offense is offense that will result in harm.

Friend: True, we don't really want to harm anyone.

Director: No, I was talking about harm to us.

Friend: Oh. But what about harm to others?

Director: If the truth harms...

Friend: ...so be it?

Director: Does it sound a little cavalier?

Friend: More than a little.

Director: If the truth causes harm... bottle it up.

Friend: No! That's ridiculous.

Director: If the truth causes harm, share it in small doses?

Friend: That's better, I suppose.

Director: Yes, they might build up a tolerance that way.

Friend: You mean they might gradually learn to think.

Director: That, too.

Friend: Is there a difference between accepting the truth and thinking the truth?

Director: I think there is. Why?

Friend: The passive can accept but never think.

Director: Hmm. Now that I think of it, don't you have to think before you accept? I mean, what does it mean to accept without thought?

Friend: It can't be true acceptance. But what does thought before acceptance take?

Director: I think we need to clear something up. What does it mean to accept?

Friend: To believe something is true.

Director: Wouldn't it be better to know something is true?

Friend: Sure, but sometimes you can't know until you believe.

Director: If that's true, how do we come to believe?

Friend: We allow ourselves to be persuaded.

Director: That sounds passive.

Friend: Maybe I should say we persuade ourselves.

Director: How do we do that?

Friend: We make up our minds.

Director: What does that mean, 'make up our minds'?

Friend: We form an opinion.

Director: How do we do that?

Friend: Oh enough! We just do, that's all.

Director: Okay, but can we see that if all of this goes into acceptance, it's best that we think our way through?

Friend: Yes. It makes sense to think when you form an opinion.

Director: But not everyone does. Some take things on authority. Others parrot the last thing they heard. And so on.

Friend: And so on. But once we accept something as true, what's to think?

Director: We have to think about the implications of this truth. Thought ramifies, you know.

Friend: I thought we wanted to keep things simple.

Director: We do. And what's simpler than the branchings in a tree?

Friend: Are you talking about logic?

Director: Logic, sure.

Friend: Logic is thought.

Director: Yes. But not all thought is logic.

Friend: If not logic, what is it?

Director: I don't know what it is. I just know what it's not.

Friend: Can you give an example?

Director: No.

Friend: Ha! You're just going to make an assertion and not back it up?

Director: That's exactly what I'm doing.

Friend: Can you at least say whether this other way of thinking is active or passive?

Director: It has elements of both.

Friend: I know what you're doing.

Director: What am I doing?

Friend: You're trying to spur thought.

Director: Both my own and others'.

Friend: It's a sort of challenge you're throwing down, to find the thought that isn't thought.

Director: As commonly understood. Here's my first guess after pondering this a while. There's a biological component to it.

Friend: I'd say there's a spiritual component to it.

Director: So we have some grounds for discussion.

Friend: Discussion is thinking out loud, a very active thing.

Director: So long as we don't give in to the temptation.

Friend: What temptation?

Director: To be agreeable.

Friend: Well, you get nowhere when you're that. You have to have the courage of your thought. You have to speak what you think. That's the only honest way. And honesty helps us find the truth.

Director: So honesty is a sort of tool?

Friend: Yes, I'd say it is. If we learn to use it well, it brings us truth.

Director: Brings us truth, or brings us to the truth?

Friend: Either way is good.

Director: Some truths are portable, others are not. We have to be—to be, I say—in a certain place to appreciate them.

Friend: Say more about that.

Director: Everyone, it seems, expects a portable truth. 'The truth should come to me.'

Friend: But sometimes we must go to the mountain.

Director: And do more than look. We must climb.

Friend: If we want the view from the heights.

Director: Yes. And you'll never know that view unless you're there.

Friend: The passive will never know. Pictures, virtual reality, whatever—they can never recreate the actual view.

Director: What do you think motivates someone to climb?

Friend: Love of truth.

Director: Maybe. What else?

Friend: Ambition.

Director: For many, yes. What else?

Friend: I don't know. To get away from the passive?

Director: Yes, I think that's true. It's often a miasma with them. The heights promise better air. But...

Friend: But what?

Director: ...maybe we're promising a passive simplification of things. From a vast distance, everyone looks the same.

Friend: Like ants.

Director: Yes, ants.

Friend: Well, we'll think about what it means to use distance as a simplification. We're aware of what we're doing.

Director: Are the passive aware they're passive?

Friend: Many of them are, sure. But not the best of them.

Director: We can shake the best of them awake?

Friend: Yes, we can.

Director: How?

Friend: There's only one way. By sharing enlivening thoughts.

37

Director: Yes, though I'm not sure if that's the only way.

Friend: What other way is there?

Director: I don't know. It might have something to do with our distinction between shaken and stirred. But maybe that's just semantics.

Friend: Maybe. Does it help if we change what we're saying a bit?

Director: How so?

Friend: Instead of the best being unaware they're passive, the best are unaware they're asleep.

Director: Aren't we all unaware that we're asleep when we're asleep?

Friend: I'm not sure. I've had dreams where I know I'm dreaming.

Director: Ah, now I remember. They call those lucid dreams.

Friend: Yes! Have you had them?

Director: I have. So what are we saying? The best have lucid dreams?

Friend: I think that's what we should say.

Director: But why?

Friend: What do you mean?

Director: What's good about knowing you're dreaming? You're still dreaming and we want you to wake.

Friend: Oh, I guess I hadn't thought that through.

Director: How do we know when someone is asleep?

Friend: Sleep as a metaphor, right?

Director: Right.

Friend: We know by talking to them.

Director: And we know because we know we're awake?

Friend: How do we know we're awake?

Director: That's the problem here, Friend. We might be talking and we're both asleep, dreaming we're awake.

Friend: I don't think there's anything to do but constantly check somehow to see if we're awake.

Director: I agree. And that's what dialogue is for.

Friend: I think the same is true about being passive.

Director: We might discover we're both passive?

Friend: Sure.

Director: But how?

Friend: We might notice something we had overlooked, something we hadn't thought about before, or given adequate thought.

Director: Yes. But what if we decide to leave that thing alone?

Friend: And give it no thought?

Director: Don't you think that happens every day?

Friend: You have a point. Most people think dialogue about the unthought-of is a waste of time. But I think it's great you bring people to think and see.

Director: It's not one-sided. They help me see more myself. It's an active hunt for us both.

Friend: But still, you bring them to see.

Director: They bring themselves. There's no bringing another to see. Each of us sees on our own.

Friend: Yes, yes, you have to say that, I know.

Director: Don't you know the unaware can make us aware we're unaware?

Friend: How?

Director: If you and I are talking, and you realize I'm unaware vanilla ice cream is best, you might wonder how you know it's best, in order to teach me. But as you wonder you realize you have no proof vanilla is best. You become aware of your ignorance on this score. And now you want to search with me for proof. Absent proof, other flavors start asserting their claims. It's a chaos of tastes, until you know that one is truly best.

Friend: Nonsense. The answer is simple. To each his own.

Director: All tastes are equally good, even when forgetting about ice cream and expanding our scope?

Friend: Well no, of course not. Some people have a taste for violence.

Director: If we include those who passively watch, I'd say it's more than 'some'.

Friend: That's true. Why do you think that is?

Director: Why does violence sell? Maybe we like to imagine ourselves as powerful? Or maybe we see it as a sort of revenge.

Friend: I just think it's titillating.

Director: That's for sex, isn't it?

Friend: Sex, violence—they're the number one sellers. I think there's some overlap here.

Director: How does this bear on the passive?

Friend: The passive prefer to watch. Rather than go out and play a violent sport, the passive watch others play.

Director: And they speak in praise of the game?

Friend: Of course. They're often great students of the game.

Director: What does it say about you if you study something you don't play?

Friend: It says you're a fan.

Director: Is fandom bad?

Friend: Not when the violence is controlled.

Director: But if the violence is total?

Friend: The fans are culpable here.

Director: But what if society as a whole accepts—no, positively supports and condones—lethal violence?

Friend: Society is to blame, as are the fans.

Director: What if everyone participates in the violence? No passive fans.

Friend: That would never happen.

Director: Why not?

Friend: The passive would be in the majority and never allow an all-involved game.

Director: I'm not so sure about the majority part. But what are we saying? Who are the active? The thinkers?

Friend: Yes. Why?

Director: Would thinkers indulge in an orgy of total violence?

Friend: I don't think they would. Would they?

Director: Here I can only tell you my opinion. And my opinion is 'no'.

Friend: Let's hope we never find out if our opinions are wrong.

Director: Let's hope we come to knowledge, and that our knowledge will set us free.

Friend: Knowledge alone won't set us free. We have to act on our knowledge. You know that.

Director: Knowledge tells us what to do. And if we know what to do, we'll often have success.

Friend: Why not always have success?

Director: There's a conflict between knowledge and success.

Friend: What conflict?

Director: It has to do with the halo effect of success. We read backwards from the success and assume there must have been worthy knowledge. That's not always the case.

Friend: Yes, but that doesn't change things. If you know what to do, you'll have success. By definition.

Director: It's that definition I challenge. Sometimes doing what you know you must do won't bring you success.

Friend: Won't bring you 'success'.

Director: We can say that, but that dilutes the meaning of success.

Friend: You want a unified meaning here?

Director: I think we need one.

Friend: Why?

Director: Look, we can say there's worldly success, and then there's true success. But I want true success to be of this world. So there's only one success here.

Friend: One success that doing-what-we-know-we must-do won't bring? Director, that makes no sense.

Director: Or it means we have to challenge what we 'know'.

Friend: Alright, I'll take your clumsy point. But now it's time for another drink.

Director: No, let's leave this celebration and go out for a walk. The weather is fine and the city is lively tonight.

Friend: Where shall we walk?

Director: Down to the harbor, so we can watch the planes as they come and go.

Friend: That sounds good to me. I've always loved it down there. No one but my niece might miss us here. And she's busy with everyone else.

* * * * * * *

PART TWO

Scene: The harbor

38

Director: Ah, the air is nice and crisp. Fall has finally come.

Friend: Many people don't look forward to the fall. Winter is too close.

Director: Really? Too bad for them. Everything is nicer when things cool down.

Friend: Can't stand the heat of activity?

Director: I prefer to be active and cool, not some sweaty mess. Besides, haven't you ever heard the saying, 'Never let them see you sweat'?

Friend: You sweat alone?

Director: I do.

Friend: Why do you think the saying is so popular? Why not sweat in front of others?

Director: I think there are a few reasons. One might be you don't want them to see they're getting to you. Another might be you don't want them to see your limits.

Friend: That's interesting about limits. But if that's what it is, what happens when it comes time to think?

Director: You do most of your thinking in private.

Friend: But what about dialogue? Don't you think then?

Director: You do. But you take more home with you to think about later than you think then.

Friend: I'm surprised you downplay it that way.

Director: Downplay? That's a high compliment. Food for thought is the rarest delight.

Friend: But you'd set the table for one?

Director: The metaphor of food is no longer useful here.

Friend: That's your old excuse whenever things don't go your way. 'The metaphor doesn't allow.'

Director: Then I'll say this. Thought is essentially private. Dialogue can spur you to think. But that's the most it can do.

Friend: We're all on our own.

Director: For this, yes. But if we get stuck we dialogue again. And so it goes.

Friend: Do you get stuck?

Director: Of course I do. More often than not. Why do you think I keep sharing words with friends? I need help.

Friend: Somehow I don't believe you.

Director: Believe what you like. But I'll tell you this. I've learned something about the passive today. Something I want to think about more.

Friend: What?

Director: It parades itself as success.

Friend: How did you learn that?

Director: Through a series of inferences based on things we've said.

Friend: I'll ask you to walk me through them another time. So how does the passive parade itself as success?

Director: The passive don't have to try. To many that seems the height of success.

Friend: Because they, the many, have to try so hard?

Director: Yes. But that's not to say they always think.

Friend: They have to try to make a living.

Director: That's right.

Friend: So you're saying the passive are rich?

Director: No, not quite that, though some of them are. But, you know, some of the rich have to make a living.

Friend: Why?

Director: Because they believe that's best. They're taught to try.

Friend: But that's good.

Director: Why?

Friend: We all have to try.

Director: Why not try to think?

Friend: Thinking is the province of the privileged class?

Director: Of course not. But if you could spend your time thinking why do something else?

Friend: Because thinking... isn't enough!

Director: But thinking and money might be enough?

Friend: What? You don't believe that.

Director: Most people want money. Yes?

Friend: Yes.

Director: And they consider that success.

Friend: True.

Director: But you and I know that's not success.

Friend: We do. The question is what you do once you're rich.

Director: And I suggest you should think. Is that so bad?

Friend: No, I guess it's not. But the poor can think.

Director: Of course they can.

Friend: So why be rich?

Director. I really don't know.

Friend: But there are a million reasons to be rich!

Director: Name one.

Friend: Better healthcare.

Director: The most important healthcare is taking care of your mind.

Friend. Well, if you're rich you can buy whatever you want.

Director: That's probably true. But how will you know what to buy without a well ordered mind?

Friend: The rich can buy on a whim.

Director: And they're passive in that. Do you disagree?

Friend: If they buy without thought? No, I agree. So you're saying the only advantage to bring rich is that you have more time to think?

Director: I'm not sure that's what I'm saying.

Friend: So you agree the rich have other advantages.

Director: No, I'm saying I'm not so sure the rich have all that much more time to think.

Friend: Ha! You think the poor have more?

Director: Maybe I'm an egalitarian. We all can have time to think. And those of us who say they can't seem to me not to want to think.

Friend: They look down on those who think.

Director: Indeed. They claim some sort of moral high ground. Work replaces thought, with them.

Friend: It's possible to think while you work.

Director: It is. And to save up kernels of thought for later when there's more time.

Friend: Ah, so you admit we need time!

Director: Of course we need time. But even if we have all the time in the world, we can't think twenty-for hours a day.

Friend: Why not?

Director: Because we get tired. And the greater the thought the more rest we need.

Friend: Some have no time for rest. Some work two jobs. Some even work more.

Director: There's still time to think. Slowly, carefully, whenever they can.

Friend: But it's unfair. They'll never have enough time to progress.

Director: Be careful here. Remember the tortoise and hare. The quick ones sometimes lose the race.

Friend: That's why the slow ones with lots of time will win!

Director: I shouldn't have mentioned a race. It's not a competition, Friend.

Friend: Competition is all the ambitious care about. They never step back and think. If they do, it's merely to think how to win.

Director: There's nothing wrong with winning, or ambition for that matter. It's when lust for victory clouds our judgment that we have a problem. Lust, emphatically, has no thought.

Friend: So what do you think about thinking how to win? Is that really thought?

Director: It sometimes seems to me that there are two kinds of thought based on two kinds of questions. The first is, 'What is it?' The second is, 'How do I...?' Answering the second without answering the first is the height of foolishness. For instance, who would want to be king without knowing what a king is?

Friend: Everyone knows what a king is.

Director: Everyone thinks they know what a king is—most everyone, at least. So let's say you manage to become king, and you realize when you do that you don't like what you see. Happy?

Friend: No, you're an unhappy king. Do you think this happens often?

Director: Maybe not with kings, but with other types of things, yes, very often. Certain careers, for instance. Before we know what they really are we set out with all our hopes and dreams to obtain them. And when we do? Not all of us are happy.

Friend: That's true.

Director: Yes, any time we think about how-do-I before what-is-it we're in for serious trouble. We think we're actively chasing our 'dream' but we're passively living an actual dream.

Friend. That's funny. People say 'living the dream' when asked how they're doing.

Director. They say it sarcastically.

Friend. They do.

Director: Do you wonder why that is?

Friend: No, I think I know.

Director: Can you explain it to me?

Friend: I think the best way to describe it is that they were at some point made a promise.

Director: Either by others or themselves?

Friend: Yes, and that's a good point. Anyway, the promise was broken. The reality of the situation is much less desirable than it was in the dream the promise conjured.

Director: They were put under a spell?

Friend: Exactly. And the spellbound are passive.

Director: I would break the spell if I could.

Friend: So would I. But that might not win us friends. No one likes to have their dream taken away.

Director: Dream, dream, dream. Why can't we call it something else?

Friend: Like what?

Director: Aspiration, or rational goal, or realistic aiming point.

Friend: Who will be inspired by 'realistic aiming point'?

Director: You might be surprised. I think there are some, an important some.

Friend: But we can't just speak to 'some'. Don't you know Napoleon's saying? 'Strike the mass, and the rest will follow—to boot!'

Director: You want to speak to the many? But what of the few, the rational, realistic few? Who will speak to them? No, I'd rather speak to those who simply aspire, not dream, no matter what their numbers might be.

Friend: You'd speak to them if they were the majority?

Director: You don't think I would?

Friend: You're a contrarian, my friend. You always support the cause of the few.

Director: I'm in permanent opposition? No, I don't think that's me.

Friend: Then what are you?

Director: I'm aware there are good regimes and bad regimes.

Friend: Ha! I struck a nerve. You bring in politics.

Director: I didn't bring them in. They always come in on their own.

Friend: What do you mean?

Director: We've been talking about different sorts of people. Politics is always a question of what sort of person will rule.

Friend: You mean who will rule.

Director: No, I mean what type of person will rule. Each regime casts a particular spell. The spellbound gather toward the throne. Sometimes one will rule, other times a few. But beware when someone fully awake approaches the throne.

Friend: Why?

Director: That marks the end of the regime.

Friend: I don't understand.

Director: Regimes are all about dreams. When a non-dreamer comes to rule, everyone is forced to wake up.

Friend: What happens then?

Director: Much good can happen then. And this might go on for two, maybe three rulers in a row. But then? The waking nightmare begins.

Friend: Why a nightmare?

Director: The regime comes apart at its seams. And with no regime...

Friend: ...there can be no good. So how can we prevent this? How can wakeful rule go on and on?

Director: It will take a great deal of luck.

Friend: That's what the ancients said.

Director: And the moderns tried to overcome luck. But overcoming luck generally involves a loss of freedom, the freedom derived from chance.

Friend: You're telling the truth.

Director: The problem with wakeful rule is that would-be rulers know no limits to their ambition.

Friend: That's a real problem. So how do we check ambition?

Director: The age old solution is to fill the heads of the ambitious with stories.

Friend: What sort of stories?

Director: Stories about the sacred nature of the regime.

Friend: What do we mean by 'regime'?

Director: A regime is the entire way of life of a group of people. In our era, it comprises state and society both—public and private entire.

Friend: A lot of people would disagree with you there.

Director: A lot of people do unthinking things. That's not my problem, Friend.

Friend: No, I agree. So are you saying the wakeful leader doesn't see the regime as sacred?

Director: Yes. And that's why he or she is dangerous. At best, the wakeful leader sees good things in the regime, things worth defending. The wakeful ruler wants to be remembered for defending the good. Can you see why it takes luck to have more than one such ruler in place?

Friend: I can. Ambition spawns dreams.

Director: True, and we can be wakeful about the regime yet live in a dream of our own. That's the real problem here.

Friend: Such dreamers, such passive thinkers, can't come to power.

Director: How can we prevent it?

Friend: I was going to ask you.

Director: We want the fully awake. Those awake concerning the regime, and those awake concerning themselves.

Friend: They need the reasonable aiming point.

Director: Indeed. And reason says to support the good.

Friend: Even at our own expense?

Director: Supporting the good is, if we're good, to support ourselves. Our leaders have to see this.

Friend: That's what they should be taught from the time they're young.

Director: Yes. The youths must want to be good so they can identify with the broader good. When asked that question, 'What do you want to be when you grow up?' the answer must be, 'I want to be good.' Nothing else matters. A regime that has such ones rule, that would be good.

Friend: But what do you mean by good?

Director: Active.

Friend: There would be thinkers in key positions.

Director: Yes.

Friend: Thinkers about what-is-rule?

Director: And what-is-good, among other things.

Friend: But they know what's good. Thinking.

Director: Thought is the primary good. But there are other goods.

Friend: Of course there are.

Director: One of the things our rulers must decide is who gets what goods and why.

Friend: They should reward the thoughtful.

Director: I agree. But things get complicated very quickly. It takes a true expert to keep an eye on the prize.

Friend: Someone skilled in all the arguments one can make on either side?

Director: Someone skilled in seeing and adhering to truth.

Friend: And good thought leads to the truth.

Director: Just as bad thought leads to the false.

Friend: You know, our regime will have its enemies.

Director. I know.

Friend: There might be times when we have to be false with them. Does that mean we want our leaders to be skilled in bad thought?

Director: Saving our nation through lies is good?

Friend: I think it is.

Director: Well, in order to lie you have to know the truth. So it's not a matter of bad thought. It's just a matter of lies.

Friend: Lying for a good cause. But what if they get a taste for lying? What if they lie to those they rule?

Director: Those they lead? Why would they?

Friend: To secure advantage for themselves.

Director: Their understood advantage is to be good. Is lying to their followers good?

Friend: Their fellow citizens, you mean? No, I don't think it's good.

Director: Why not?

Friend: Lies are bad input for thought.

Director: Ah, a very good point. But what if lies make you think?

Friend: Well....

Director: Yes 'well'. Do I dare say it? Lies are good if they make you think. There, I've done it.

Friend: You don't believe that.

Director: No I don't. But maybe it made you think just a little?

Friend: A little.

Director: That's all I ask.

39

Friend: Do you want to know what it made me think?

Director: I do.

Friend: It made me think that lies are active.

Director: Are they?

Friend: I don't know. I tend to think they're passive.

Director: Why?

Friend: Because they take no effort.

Director: I don't know about that. Lies take effort to live. Maybe even more effort than the truth.

Friend: How so?

Director: The only way to truly live a lie is to construct a whole world that supports it. You have to live that whole world. You never get to rest. But the truth makes a good, hard bed to sleep on.

Friend: You know, that's true. But then are we saying telling the truth is passive?

Director: Hush! Of course not. Don't you know it can be very hard to tell the truth?

Friend: Certainly.

Director: Well, ask any truth teller how passive a thing it is.

Friend: I take your point. But what about when it's easy? Are we saying the only activity is hard activity?

Director: You bring us to the crux. Is thinking always hard?

Friend: I... don't know.

Director: When would it be easy?

Friend: When we think about simple things.

Director: No. The simple things can be very hard to master.

Friend: Is that what thinking is about? Mastery?

Director: Well, it's not about slavery.

Friend: What's it about?

Director: Knowledge.

Friend: We actively gain knowledge. But memorizing the phone book gives us knowledge.

Director: There's knowledge, and then there's useful knowledge.

Friend: So thinking is about the useful. We actively pursue the useful. I like that.

Director: Good. You're not afraid of self-interest in thought.

Friend: But I thought thought was objective.

Director: The objective always seeks its objective. And its objective is its interest.

Friend: If I didn't think you were just making all of this up I'd say that's very true.

Director: Even if I'm making it up, if it's true it's true.

Friend: When you're making things up, are you active or passive?

Director: I have to think what to say. So, active, of course.

Friend: Is it harder to make things up or tell the truth?

Director: Is it harder to lift heavy weights or run very fast? They're simply two different things. Sometimes harder, sometimes easier.

Friend: But very hard if you push yourself to the extreme.

Director: It's always hard to push yourself. Isn't it?

Friend: Of course it is. Activity is a push. Passivity is lying still.

Director: Yes, but sometimes we need to be still.

Friend: When?

Director: When listening for precious things.

Friend: What precious things?

Director: From the lips of others.

Friend: Well yes, that's true. You don't want to scare them off.

Director: But let's not say precious things need us to be passive.

Friend: What do they need?

Director: Active concern. Being gentle takes a good amount of effort, doesn't it? And aren't we gentle when we're actively concerned?

Friend: Of course we are. I'd even say being rough is a sign of lack of concern.

Director: I don't know about that. Sometimes people are rough or sharp because they don't know any better. They do care, or so it seems to me.

Friend: Point taken. Caring isn't enough.

Director: But being gentle isn't enough either. We must act once we learn precious things.

Friend: Act in what way?

Director: We must speak well-chosen words.

Friend. To speak is to act?

Director: Only when the listener takes the words to heart.

Friend: I suppose you'd say to write is to act.

Director: In the same way, but at a remove.

Friend: Writing is more cowardly than speaking.

Director: I think it's best to say the two complement one another. The written word can prepare you for a spoken word. And the other way round.

Friend: How so 'prepare'?

Director: Make you aware of something you might not have otherwise noticed.

Friend: I thought we can't make another aware. I thought it's up to them.

Director: And it is. But sometimes they need a key.

Friend: To unlock their own heart so they can take in the words? Do you know how arrogant that sounds?

Director: Then is love arrogant?

Friend: Ha! Now you want to hide behind love!

Director: Who's hiding? I'm front and center when it comes to love.

Friend: What does that mean?

Director: When I'm in love, I say it. I let it be known.

Friend: Yes, but not to the person you love.

Director: But with my love I try with all my might.

Friend: Try to do what? Argue philosophy with them?

Director: 'Argue' sounds so negative. No, I'll make sweet sounding speeches, delightful discourse, lovely logos.

Friend: But why love?

Director: That's the best way to understanding.

Friend: Active understanding?

Director: Active understanding.

Friend: Which amounts to mutual love.

Director: Yes.

Friend: What is it you love in the other?

Director: Their soul.

Friend: You know, I actually believe you. What kind of soul are you looking for?

Director: A lively soul. One with a spark, if not a flame.

Friend: What are the spark and flame?

Director: The sparks are flashes of understanding. The flame is knowledge.

Friend: Knowledge in the soul. I like that. Is that active?

Director: Here I want to say something I may go against later. Knowledge is beyond activity or passivity. Knowledge just is.

Friend: And so the soul just is?

Director: Soul is more complicated than that. The soul can be active or passive.

Friend: Active when understanding flashes?

Director: Yes. And passive when it doesn't.

Friend: So souls are mostly passive? I mean, we don't have flashes of understanding all the time.

Director: Oh, you'd be surprised. Some souls are flashing all the time, like fireflies in the night.

Friend: And what, they live from flash of understanding to flash of understanding?

Director: They do.

Friend: But that's a pointless life! Just wandering from flash to flash.

Director: Is it pointless? I don't know. It sounds pretty good to me.

Friend: But we need to have an aim, a plan. We need to accomplish something with our lives.

Director: Some people use knowledge for that.

Friend: You can't build with a flame.

Director: Can you build in the dark?

Friend: Okay, you have a point. But let's not take this metaphor too far.

Director: That's always good advice. So where are we?

Friend: On the edge of the water, contemplating the night.

Director: Does any good come of our contemplation?

Friend: It can prepare us to act.

Director: I think that's true. It's like the sleep that prepares us for the day.

Friend: No, it's not like that at all.

Director: What's it like?

Friend: The food that gives us the energy we need.

Director: I like that, too. Food for thought. Right?

Friend: Exactly.

Director: Do you know what I like to contemplate?

Friend: Tell me.

Director: Words. Words, words, words.

Friend: What about deeds?

Director: There's often not much to contemplate there. But what someone says about a deed? Ah, that's usually rich to ponder.

Friend: You like it when word and deed don't match?

Director: I'm not sure I 'like' it. But I find it fascinating. And I like to speak up when I can.

Friend: What do you say? 'Your words don't match your deed?'

Director: I'm not often that blunt. It takes a delicate touch. After all, it's not all the time you can call someone a liar to their face.

Friend: Are we liars when our words don't match our deeds? What if we don't know any better?

Director: I think when we act we all know, on some level. I like to remind people of that knowledge.

Friend: You're assuming you can match the words to the deed. You're assuming you know better.

Director: This is what I've always concerned myself with, from earliest years on up. I have expertise here. Do I assume I know better? No. That's why I question. That's what dialogue is for. But if it's clear there's a poor match, and I don't think the effort will be fruitless, I speak.

Friend: But how 'fruitless'?

Director: I just mean I don't speak when I don't think speaking will do any good.

Friend: What makes you think that?

Director: When the person shows no sign of concern with justice.

Friend: Justice? I don't understand. Why justice?

Director: What do you think justice is?

Friend: Getting what you deserve.

Director: Well, certain deeds deserve certain words. Don't you think?

Friend: I think that's true. So you only speak to those who want the right words.

Director: Yes. We look for them together. But for those who don't care about words? Why should I bother with them?

Friend: The right words are food for the soul.

Director: I couldn't have said it any better myself.

Friend: But some people don't nourish their soul.

Director: That's true. And why should they? Their naked deeds get them what they want.

Friend: Their unjust deeds.

Director: I agree. Without true words deeds are unjust.

Friend: But true words aren't some magic powder you sprinkle on a deed.

Director: Of course they're not. True words proceed from very true deeds.

Friend: You have to say more about that.

Director: There are deeds that are called for, and there are deeds that are uncalled for. The called for deeds are true.

Friend: But who calls for the deeds?

Director: Would you believe me if I said the universe?

Friend: No.

Director: Then I'll tell you that the true-hearted call for these deeds.

Friend: I believe that. They call with all their might.

Director: And the good, the good-hearted, listen to this call. And then they act.

Friend: They think?

Director: They think, and then they act in deed.

Friend: But to think is a deed.

Director: They think, and then they act with a second order deed.

Friend: I wonder how many great actors throughout history would appreciate being called second order actors?

Director: I don't think some of them would mind. After all, truly great second order action requires great primary order thought.

Friend: Then why do they want to be known for the secondary?

Director: Sometimes that's all the choice they have.

Friend: They lived in an age where primary order thought wasn't appreciated?

Director: That happens often, you know. But we may be living in a special time, where light shines down upon the primary. After all, isn't that what our conversation has been about? Would such a conversation be possible in any other time?

Friend: How would I know? But are you saying we should be famous for this?

Director: Known, not famous. Known by those who know.

Friend: What happens when those who know are the majority? Have we seen that before?

Director: It's very hard to say. Suffice it to say, I don't know.

40

Friend: What would it take to know?

Director: You'd have to be there, and converse with many.

Friend: What about today? Do many know?

Director: Know thought? I'm inclined to say yes.

Friend: So they can recognize thought.

Director: Yes.

Friend: Then our outlook is good!

Director: Just because you can recognize thought doesn't mean you're a supporter of thought.

Friend: Why wouldn't you be?

Director: Because that takes courage. And courage is always in short supply.

Friend: Why do you say 'always'? Why can't there be courageous times?

Director: There can be. But I think if you ask anyone who was there, they'd say they'd like to have had a little more courage, please.

Friend: There's never enough. That makes sense. And the passive are cowardly.

Director: The passive are cowardly.

Friend: If we could only get them to think.

Director: Yes. And what makes matters worse is that if the times are courageous, they rebel against the times.

Friend: But isn't rebellion active?

Director: Not always.

Friend: But to rebel is to push away. Pushing, mental pushing, is active.

Director: If 'push' is what they truly do, perhaps.

Friend: You know, it's funny. Talk of pushing makes me think of giving birth.

Director: There are mental births—artworks and such. They're active, no?

Friend: Of course they are.

Director: But sometimes a more beautiful birth is a quiet word spoken at just the right time.

Friend: I agree.

Director: We give a word like that a very gentle push, just enough to get it out of our mouth, off of our lips.

Friend: Active doesn't mean frenzied.

Director: No, not at all. Active can mean calm, measured, delicate.

Friend: That's the best activity. Why aren't more people active that way?

Director: Something interferes with their thought, or so I think.

Friend: What interferes?

Director: I think it varies. But have you ever heard the phrase 'you have a bee in your bonnet'?

Friend: I have. It means you're obsessed with something.

Director: I think it also means you have something stinging you in the head, interrupting your thought. You need to get rid of the bee. But instead of focusing on that, people lash out.

Friend: We need to help them remove the bee.

Director: Not so easy when they're flailing about.

Friend: What can we do?

Director: Sometimes these people are in positions of leadership. That's very bad for those beneath them. The only thing we can do is resist when they're making no sense.

Friend: Not so easy to do.

Director: No, not so easy. But it must be done. In doing this we have to find a way to urge them to examine themselves in order to see what the problem really is.

Friend: They don't know they have a bee?

Director: Sometimes they don't know what it is. They just know they're being stung. But sometimes they do know what it is but refuse to address it.

Friend: Why?

Director: They might be afraid of bees. Or they might think the bee is doing them good, lashing them onwards toward success.

Friend: It's funny, but I think you might be right. How can we convince them that either bees are nothing to be afraid of, or that getting stung isn't good?

Director: It seems to me the same approach is called for in either case. We must speak in praise of thought.

Friend: That's it?

Director: What did you expect? If they want to think badly enough, they might take action to make that possible.

Friend: Kill the bee.

Director: Or just let it out. It probably doesn't want to be there, anyway.

Friend: True. You know, I think there are times when a whole nation can have a bee in its bonnet. Do you take the same approach then?

Director: Of course. You just have to pitch it on a broader scale.

Friend: You mean you have to write.

Director: That's usually the way, though there are others. You can get on television, and so on. The point is that you have to try, even if it seems you're not getting through. If you can connect with one, that's success.

Friend: You tell yourself that so you don't give up.

Director: If you know of something better to tell myself, please fill me in. Success is largely how we define it. That's my definition, reaching one other. What's yours?

Friend: Well, I never really thought of one before.

Director: So you don't care that much about success?

Friend: No, of course I do.

Director: You just don't like to think about it much.

Friend: No, I think about it. I just don't define it to myself.

Director: Define it to me.

Friend: Success is.... Oh, this is pointless. You're the philosopher. Give me a definition.

Director: But I gave you a definition.

Friend: That's your definition.

Director: No, it's everyone's definition. Doesn't everyone want to reach another sometime in their life? And if you reach more than one, so much the better. Or, rather, that's equally good.

Friend: No, you don't mean that. Reaching more is better, not equally as good as reaching one.

Director: I disagree. Quality, not quantity, counts here.

Friend: Reaching ten with full quality is better than reaching one with full quality.

Director: Again, I disagree.

Friend: Why? More is better!

Director: Let me share an assumption I'm making. The message is tailored for one. Full quality is reached only with that one. Everyone else gets a sort of diluted word.

Friend: Then tailor your message for each one you meet.

Director: Ah, but then that dilutes the effect with the first one.

Friend: Don't let that one know about the other ones.

Director: You'd have me be dishonest?

Friend: I'm not saying that. Be a tailor. That's what I'm saying.

Director: You'd have me rework my whole life's philosophy for each one I meet? Impossible. There can be only one.

Friend: You surprise me. You're usually not this adamant.

Director: Being asked the impossible rouses me every time.

Friend: Well, I'm sorry for asking you the impossible. So have you reached your one?

Director: I don't know.

Friend: How can you not know? Won't what you say resonate so strongly that it'll be obvious?

Director: Oh, I've had resonance on many occasions. But did it go to the core? And did something develop in that core? I don't know. These things take time.

Friend: How much time?

Director: Years, sometimes a lifetime.

Friend: So you might never know?

Director: I might never know.

Friend: How can you go on not knowing?

Director: How can any of us go on not knowing?

Friend: We take it on faith. But I find it hard to believe that you, as a philosopher, would say that.

Director: What do you think I'd say?

Friend: That you see no other way.

41

Director: I can see other ways, but they all look bad.

Friend: Bad for you. Or will you say they're bad for everyone?

Director: That's the real question here. We're often taught that everyone must find their own way. This implies that all ways, provided they truly belong to someone, are good. So what if these other ways I see, the ones that look bad, belong to others?

Friend: You can steer clear and leave them be. But you beg the question.

Director: What question?

Friend: Whether there isn't a way for all, or some subset of all.

Director: Two is a subset of all.

Friend: Yes, but I'm talking about something more—something greater.

Director: What have you got in mind?

Friend: Philosophy.

Director: Yes, but I have some serious doubts.

Friend: What doubts?

Director: Not everyone is suited for philosophy.

Friend: That's what makes it a subset of all. But what do you need to be suited?

Director: You have to start out as a quick learner with a good memory.

Friend: And then?

Director: You have to care about justice and ideas. Not everyone cares much about these things, you know.

Friend: I know. What else?

Director: Those are the basic ingredients. But there is something more, something that's very hard to describe. It's a sort of longing, a deep and urgent longing.

Friend: For what?

Director: That's the thing. It isn't clear. Philosophy helps make it clear.

Friend: If philosophy can make it clear, it can put it in so many words. So what are the words?

Director: You'll think I'm cheating if I tell you that it goes beyond all words. You do believe there are things beyond words, don't you?

Friend: Of course I do. But are you saying this is simply something you know when you see it?

Director: Yes, but you have to know what you're looking for.

Friend: Say what you're looking for.

Director: Often times there's a sort of clumsy bashfulness, a tripping over one's feet in words. This comes from a strong desire to do justice to the truth one feels inside.

Friend: Why bashful?

Director: Not all are bashful. But when someone is, it's usually because they can sense they're not doing justice to what they feel.

Friend: So do you bring them outside themselves?

Director: You've hit it on the head. They have to step out of the inner darkness and into the outer light.

Friend: Assuming it's not night.

Director: Yes, that's true. But if they can step out right at high noon, with little shadow to be seen, they get a better sense of what exactly justice is. This gives them much to think about as they return inside themselves.

Friend: How much to think about?

Director: Sometimes enough for a lifetime of activity.

Friend: Thought.

Director: Yes, but other actions as well—speaking and writing, which of course can involve much thought. And other things.

Friend: Well, we all have to speak. But few of us write. So that alone means philosophy isn't for all.

Director: Not all philosophers write. And not all who write are philosophers.

Friend: Not even if they're very active, thoughtful writers?

Director: Thinking alone does not make you a philosopher. Otherwise we'd have to say that all activity is philosophy. Do you want to say that?

Friend: Of course not.

Director: The point is that philosophy is something more, something beyond thinking.

Friend: Communicating thought.

Director: Yes, loosely speaking. Communication. We communicate philosophically.

Friend: But what does that mean?

Director: We share the process of breaking down ideas into their components, in a sense.

Friend: And then we can build them back up into better ideas.

Director: That's what often happens. But now I'm not happy with what I said. Sharing a process. Philosophy is hardly a process.

Friend: Let me guess. You go by feel.

Director: That's a very good guess. Feel tempered by thought.

Friend: You feel the ideas.

Director: Does that surprise you?

Friend: Yes. Who ever heard of philosophy feeling ideas?

Director: You just ask, 'How does this idea make me feel?' And then you think.

Friend: You think maybe the idea is good and there's something bad in you that makes you feel bad?

Director: Or the other way round. The point is that the feeling is a point of departure for analysis.

Friend: But everyone feels differently.

Director: There are different feelings, yes. But they are shared by many in most cases.

Friend: So you should focus where you feel differently than the rest.

Director: Focus on that and see where it leads. That's the adventure. That's your own way.

Friend: And if you meet others who share your feelings?

Director: Then you have friends.

42

Friend: And if you never find anyone who shares your feelings?

Director: You carry on and look for the one.

Friend: You've never met anyone who shares your feelings?

Director: I've met plenty of people who share some of my feelings.

Friend: Some but not all.

Director: 'All' is only possible for fleeting moments at best. 'Some' is what we live with every day.

Friend: That's so sad.

Director: Not really. We can have great fun organizing our lives in order to maximize the 'some' while keeping open for 'all'. That's the game of life. And I'm an eager player.

Friend: How many fleeting 'alls' have you had?

Director: Several times I thought I was on the verge of all, only to be disappointed.

Friend: You've never had an all?

Director: No, but I think it's possible. And even if it isn't, I enjoy coming close.

Friend: I don't think you want an all.

Director: What? Why not?

Friend: I get the sense you're keeping something locked up inside.

Director: What could I keep locked up?

Friend: I don't know. But it has something to do with philosophy. What is philosophy?

Director: The love of wisdom.

Friend: No, don't give me that. What is it?

Director: The attempt to replace belief with knowledge.

Friend: No. What?

Director: I don't know. You tell me.

Friend: Philosophy wants to make others think a certain way.

Director: Philosophy as system of thought, and such?

Friend: Yes. Philosophy wants to own the future through thought.

Director: Philosophy as mental architecture.

Friend: Exactly!

Director: Then don't go into a building my followers build—because it will fall down! I'm no architect, no builder of minds.

Friend: What are you?

Director: Maybe I'm a plumber.

Friend: A plumber? Ha!

Director: Why laugh at that? Don't you know plumbers are necessary and good? Who keeps the pipes open? Who stops the leaks?

Friend: This takes us back to communication. Leaks. You have a secret teaching. And you'll have no leaks.

Director: If I had a secret teaching no leaks would be good. But I have no such teaching, Friend.

Friend: You just keep it from me because we don't share enough feelings.

Director: We share much. And you know it. I'm willing to share all I know about philosophy with you. But I know precious little.

Friend: And is that 'little' active?

Director: Very.

Friend: Active doing what?

Director: Thinking and sharing what I think. Just look at all we've said today!

Friend: Okay, you have a point. I'm sorry I got a little funny with you just now.

Director: That's alright. It happens to all of us from time to time. It's part of the longing, longing for truth.

Friend: You know, I've never put it that way to myself before. But I think you're right. Could I be... a philosopher?

Director: Why not? All you have to do is be willing to think about everything, then actually think about everything, then share your thoughts, and be willing to think some more.

Friend: That's really it? It sounds too simple.

Director: 'Simple' doesn't mean easy. Simple can be very, very hard.

Friend: I believe it. But why is it so hard?

Director: When it's hard it's because of pressure.

Friend: What sort of pressure?

Director: External pressure. The pressure of expectations.

Friend: Yes, I understand. Expectations are passive, aren't they?

Director: Now I'm learning. I never thought about it that way before. Can you say more?

Friend: When we expect, we don't think and then know, truly know, that something will happen. We hope or believe it should or will.

Director: But if we know something will happen?

Friend: There's no hope or belief. There is the flame of knowledge burning in our soul.

Director: Isn't hope often depicted as a sort of flame, a candle burning in the night?

Friend: Yes, that's true. Maybe I'm not as good a philosopher as I thought.

Director: Don't say that. Just be willing to keep on going. So let's consider this further. Maybe hope is like knowledge. Or better, maybe hope is incipient knowledge, the seed of knowledge.

Friend: That's intriguing. But not all seeds sprout.

Director: True. Science sometimes leads us down blind alleys.

Friend: Science? Philosophy is science?

Director: There's a great deal of overlap. But not all scientists know this, nor do all would-be philosophers. But to get back to our topic, knowledge and hope are related, if only for the simple reason that when we pursue a subject we hope to come to knowledge.

Friend: Does it work the other way?

Director: Do we know in order to hope? Yes, I think that works. Knowledge, the flame, gives us hope. It lights our way. We can't make all of this too exact, but in broad strokes it works.

Friend: Hope is active when it supports our quest.

Director: The quest makes the hope active. Without it hope is passive.

Friend: You have to do something with your hope.

Director: You have to do something with all of you or you're passive.

Friend: What's part of 'all of you'?

Director: Your desires.

Friend: What can you do with your desires?

Director: Harness them. Make them serve the cause.

Friend: The cause is the quest?

Director: The quest is the cause.

Friend: How do we harness desire?

Director: It's simple, really. Posit the cause as the end and the desire as the means.

Friend: Is that what you do?

Director: Sure. I had a desire to talk to you tonight. And the end of our talk is the cause.

Friend: The end of your talk is always the cause.

Director: I gather all my desires up into one. I satisfy them and my larger hopes, too.

Friend: Isn't that a little too single minded?

Director: I like to call it 'focused'.

Friend: What if a desire doesn't support the cause? What if it's some errant passive desire?

Director: I re-evaluate the cause.

Friend: Really? I find that surprising.

Director: The desire is a fact. The cause takes into account all the facts. I hope to come to know the desire for what it is, then press it into service.

Friend: You wouldn't fight the desire?

Director: 'Harness' and 'fight' are two different things. The former has better effect.

Friend: Why?

Director: If you conquer your desire, you've killed a part of you. You're less than you were. And if you fight but don't conquer, you engage in a protracted enervating struggle.

Friend: But not all desires are good.

Director: When they serve the cause they're transformed. They no longer have a bad object.

Friend: Ah, the object! That's the thing. Change the object and transform. Transformation is active.

Director: It certainly is. And it happens in thought.

Friend: Thought is meatier than I gathered.

Director: Did you think thought is some airy thing? Thought engages the real, sometimes in a visceral way. All the complex intellectual systems in the world are of no use unless they can grapple with fundamental desire.

Friend: By 'grapple' you mean fight?

Director: I mean wrestle into shape.

Friend: That's what philosophy does? It wrestles into shape?

Director: In part, yes.

Friend: What's the other part?

Director: It clears away thoughts that have hardened and block the way. Thoughts should be supple, living things—not stonework in mind or soul.

Friend: Beautiful cathedrals are built with stone.

Director: The metaphor only goes so far.

43

Friend: But I think we're saying something important. If we want to build we need hard materials.

Director: For actual building, yes. But who wants to build in the mind?

Friend: Haven't you heard of the constructs of the imagination?

Director: Castles of sand in the sky.

Friend: Oh, don't be so dismissive. Aren't you impressed with great art?

Director: Of course I am. Art that makes you think.

Friend: Is that your sole criterion for great art?

Director: What else would it be?

Friend: Sometimes we want art to take us away.

Director: If art did that it would definitely make me think!

Friend: But the point is that sometimes we don't want to think.

Director: Yes, I've noticed.

Friend: Do you always want to think?

Director: I do, except when I need a rest.

Friend: But that's when you let art take you away.

Director: I want my art to bring me back, not take me away.

Friend: Bring you back where?

Director: Home.

Friend: When people say 'take me away', I think that's what they mean.

Director: Maybe some do, but many don't.

Friend: Why do you think that is?

Director: Some would say home is where you feel good. But many don't have a home like this.

Friend: I don't believe it. We all have a home like that. We just have to find it again.

Director: We disagree, my friend. Many search far and wide for home, not even knowing what it is.

Friend: Then why do they search?

Director: They intuit that an active search might lead them where they want to be.

Friend: They don't know where they want to be?

Director: They don't know. But they find clues along the way, clues that give them hope and urge them on.

Friend: Does philosophy give you clues?

Director: It does. And sometimes it brings me home.

Friend: Why not just stay at home when you find it?

Director: In a sense, I do. But there's also something passive here, something to overcome.

Friend: Inertia.

Director: Complacency, yes. Our homes need fresh air. And with fresh air come new ideas. And so it starts all over again.

Friend: The hunt for our home.

Director: Yes, and I know the metaphor is strained but it's the best I can do right now.

Friend: I think you're doing pretty well. But can't you, can't philosophy, build homes for others?

Director: And have them passively occupy the dwelling? What good would that do?

Friend: It would give them shelter from storms.

Director: Such houses fall down with the slightest of winds.

Friend: Not if they're made of stone.

Director: What does stone mean to you, Friend?

Friend: Hard and fast opinions that are true.

Director: You distinguish opinion from knowledge?

Friend: Of course I do. And knowledge goes in opinion's stone hearth to burn the night away.

Director: Burn away the night. A curious phrase. And we're saying knowledge is the wood?

Friend: We are.

Director: I'd rather we said something else.

Friend: What should we say?

Director: The firewood is dead and dried up opinion.

Friend: Opinions as trees?

Director: Yes. They grow where the soil is good and they can attain great height. But when they're dead, they burn.

Friend: And sometimes the forest catches fire.

Director: Sometimes for sure. And that's a true calamity.

Friend: So it's best to keep opinion alive.

Director: The forest keeps itself alive. The best we can do is clear the dead wood.

Friend: That's what philosophy does.

Director: In part, yes.

Friend: You always answer 'in part'.

Director: It's very hard to articulate the whole.

Friend: Try your best now with me.

Director: But I am. Sometimes it's necessary to approach the whole obliquely.

Friend: Because I wouldn't understand?

Director: Because of the nature of philosophy.

Friend: It's protean?

Director: In one sense. But in another it's always absolutely the same.

Friend: It's a paradox.

Director: It can be.

Friend: When isn't it?

Director: When it's fully known. But that suggests I fully know. I don't. But I've caught enough glimpses to suspect what I'm saying is true.

Friend: Well, it makes sense enough to me. Paradox clears up with understanding. And I've understood something important tonight.

Director: What?

Friend: That you know less than I thought!

Director: Then we've done some good after all. Correcting mistaken opinion is part of philosophy's work.

Friend: You don't mind that I don't think as highly of you?

Director: To think 'highly' is to miss the mark. I'd rather you knew me for what I am.

Friend: You still know more than anyone I know.

Director: Then you don't know the right people, Friend. I really don't know that much.

Friend: But what you know is key.

44

Director: Key to my heart, perhaps.

Friend: Do you know your heart?

Director: I like to think I know it very well. But there are surprises along the way.

Friend: What kind of surprises?

Director: The kind that make me question what I think I know, the truth about my heart.

Friend: What's a truth you've learned?

Director: Ah, that's private, my friend. Haven't you learned truths about your heart?

Friend: I have. And you're right—that's not to share. We have to guard our heart.

Director: Because it's so vulnerable?

Friend: Precisely.

Director: But there are times we can share. You do know that, don't you?

Friend: I do. We open our heart.

Director: Fully?

Friend: With the right person? Why not?

Director: How can I not agree? But the other must share in full, as well?

Friend: Of course. That's what lovers do. They share their hopes and dreams.

Director: Oh. I thought we were talking about thought.

Friend: 'Hopes and dreams' is just a phrase. We can say we share our thought.

Director: But now I feel like everything is starting to slip away. Hopes and dreams and thoughts are surely different things.

Friend: If this is how you share, you're going to have a hard time with love.

Director: But you know that's how I share. I engage. I want a dialogue with my love.

Friend: Dialogue is fine when you get together every so often as we do. But every minute of every day with your love? That love can't last. Not even friendship can last.

Director: I have to find the right love, find the right friend.

Friend: I'm afraid that friend will be in your imagination.

Director: Or memory.

Friend: You had such a friend?

Director: No, but if I find one, and you're right that the dialogue can't last, I'll enjoy it while I can and store up precious memories.

Friend: Which you'll passively enjoy.

Director: No. I'll have a dialogue with myself, with what I learned from my friend. That's the best way to honor the memory.

Friend: But that dialogue will be imaginary.

Director: Then thought is imaginary, too—which it's not.

Friend: How do you know?

Director: Ah, you put the question. I know it's not because when I communicate thought it has effect.

Friend: And if you write down your dialogues with yourself in honor of your friend?

Director: That, too, will have effect because it's crystallized thought. Thought that can be returned to again and again. Better than live conversation in certain ways. Your memory of a conversation might morph over the years. But if I write out a dialogue for you, you can return to it again and again forever, so to speak, and know that it will never change.

Friend: We can measure our progress that way.

Director: Truly. And there will be times when you swear you're not reading the same dialogue. But you know you are. That says much about how much we can change.

Friend: But you're assuming something.

Director: What?

Friend: That the reader takes the dialogue to heart, and stores certain things up in precious memory.

Director: Yes, I am assuming that. Should I?

Friend: I don't know. What if I read a dialogue and it makes me think, but I take nothing precious away from it?

Director: Maybe it will make you think again some years later. But I don't know, Friend. I tend to remember the things that make me think. Don't you?

Friend: Well, you have a point. But not everyone does.

Director: Why do you think that is?

Friend: They're ungrateful.

Director: I think you're saying something profound. Memory and gratitude go hand in hand.

Friend: But you know that's not true. I can remember someone who punched me in the nose. But I'm not grateful to him.

Director: Or her. But I take the point. Maybe only good memories have to do with gratitude. And it's good to be made to think.

Friend: That's your opinion. Not everyone shares it.

Director: If you think it's bad, or painful—or whatever—to think, you won't be grateful? That makes sense. So we're looking for those who love to think. Who actively seek opportunity to think. Who organize their lives around the drive to thought.

Friend: You really organize your life around the drive to thought?

Director: I do. And I think everyone should, as well.

Friend: We're not all made for philosophy but we're all made to think?

Director: Yes. That's what humans do.

Friend: Those who don't think aren't human?

Director: Are they?

Friend: I think you have a point. The just-following-orders crowd.

Director: Them, and there are others, too. Those who rebel at every command.

Friend: What's wrong with that? It shows independence.

Director: It's unreasonable to refuse reasonable commands. I think this is hard for many of us to hear. But there are times when others know better than we. And we should obey.

Friend: Obey? We should never obey.

Director: Maybe I should have said we should listen to reason.

Friend: Of course we should listen to reason. But that doesn't mean to obey.

Director: I obey reason. Do you?

Friend: I reason and listen to myself.

Director: Don't you obey yourself?

Friend: To obey is passive!

Director: Not to listen to reason is passive.

Friend: Why do you equate listening with obeying?

Director: Because I refuse to listen to the unreasonable.

Friend: That's not a very good answer.

Director: It's the best one I have.

Friend: Why are you fixed on 'obey'?

Director: Why are you fixed against it? You obey the law, don't you?

Friend: That's not the same thing.

Director: I think it's much the same thing. Reason is a sort of law.

Friend: And that's a flaw in reason.

Director: Again, I think you've said the profound.

Friend: How so?

Director: If reason becomes law it might harden into stone.

Friend: But you said we should obey reason.

Director: Reason, but not necessarily reason as law.

Friend: This is crazy. If not reason as law, what is law? Don't you want reason in law?

Director: Of course I do. And now I'm confused.

Friend: Ha! I've never seen you confused. What's the trouble?

Director: I think reason-as-law is better than reason-in-law.

Friend: Again, how so?

Director: In the same way as mothers are better than mothers-in-law.

Friend: Now you're teasing. And look at you smile!

Director: Alright, a little tease just now is good, I think. Mothers-in-law can be better than mothers, depending.

Friend: Depending on what?

Director: How reasonable they are.

Friend: I think that's true.

Director: It is. But not everyone sees it this way. They stick to their unreasonable mothers, come what may.

Friend: Okay, but what does this have to do with law?

Director: People stick to unreasonable laws, come what may.

Friend: That's true. So what can we do?

Director: Everything we've talked about tonight.

Friend: And what if people are still on the fence?

Director: Activity always breaks the tie.

Friend: Funny you put it that way. The Vice President breaks the ties in the Senate. But we have no Vice President here. We only have reason—and philosophy.

45

Director: Are you saying philosophers are vice presidents of sorts?

Friend: Why not?

Director: They go around breaking ties?

Friend: Fifty-fifty gets you nowhere fast.

Director: Yes. Hmm.

Friend: What are you hmm-ing about?

Director: We don't vote directly for a vice president. We vote for the ticket.

Friend: What's interesting about that?

Director: Philosophy can ride in someone else's wake.

Friend: But that's passive.

Director: Passive with an opportunity to be active if elected.

Friend: A chrysalis of sorts.

Director: Yes, but forget I said anything about it. It's patently false. Philosophy is active through and through.

Friend: And philosophy doesn't need to be elected.

Director: Not at all. Philosophy is election-proof.

Friend: But it's not majority-proof.

Director: Why not?

Friend: Because majorities can work harm on philosophy.

Director: I don't think that's true. Look at the first political philosopher, Socrates. The majority did its best to work its harm on him, and he turned out a saint.

Friend: Are you in favor of saints?

Director: You're more a philosopher than you know. I think we can do without Saint Socrates. He's doing more harm than good.

Friend: How?

Director: It has to do with Ideas, and Soul.

Friend: I always thought Plato ascribed those notions to him, that Socrates didn't really hold them.

Director: And I think you thought right. But either way, Plato and Socrates are no longer human. They have become Western Ideas. And we have to break them down. I'm not the first to say this. But that doesn't mean I don't have my work to do here.

Friend: But the modern academy is based on them.

Director: Then upturn that academy, Friend.

Friend: And leave us with what?

Director: A fresh new start.

Friend: But you're a Platonist!

Director: Should I tell you I love Plato and Socrates more than I care to say? But we need to put them to sleep.

Friend: Euthanasia?

Director: In the best possible sense.

Friend: And yet you were talking about dialogues before.

Director: Isn't emulation a mark of love?

Friend: What other philosophers do you love?

Director: I'll take a philosopher wherever and whenever I can find them.

Friend: But philosophers say such very different things.

Director: My love is strong enough for that.

Friend: Do you love Xenophon?

Director: By asking I think you know many think he's no philosopher at all.

Friend: Is he to you?

Director: It doesn't matter what title I give him.

Friend: Philosopher as a title.

Director: That's what it's become. And I've thought about this, and will think some more. Should I abandon the word 'philosopher' and strike out for something new?

Friend: Should you?

Director: I don't know. But for now, 'philosopher' it is.

Friend: You need the history of that word to support you.

Director: I need to overturn the history of that word. Using the word can help me in this.

Friend: I thought you loved philosophy.

Director: I do. And that's why I would scrape the barnacles off her hull.

Friend: Socrates and Plato are barnacles?

Director: Not the actual men, but the ideas of them. I want to strip away their fame.

Friend: And replace it with your own?

Director: I'm willing to make that sacrifice.

Friend: Ha!

Director: Fame is a passive thing. Who wants that?

Friend: Everyone!

Director: It's a prejudice that everyone wants fame. It simply isn't true. Some of the most interesting people I've met want no fame. Do you?

Friend: Well, if I could have it without the fuss....

Director: Oh, don't say that. You're really saying it isn't worth it to you.

Friend: I'm not good enough for fame. There you have it.

Director: I'm sorry that's how you feel. But are you sure you choose not to have it? Could you be famous?

Friend: I wouldn't know how.

Director: If you did know, would you?

Friend: Honestly? It seems like trouble to me.

Director: And it is. But so is life. We have to pick our trouble, Friend. Mine is philosophy.

Friend: Philosophy is truly trouble to you?

Director: Do you think it's fun picking on the things that people say?

Friend: I thought it was for you.

Director: It's a sort of duty I live.

Friend: You have no fun?

Director: I have fun with friends like you. But with everyone else? What fun in seeming strange?

Friend: I bet you do seem strange.

Director: Thank you, I think. What's that song? 'People are strange, when you're a stranger.' Well, people are strange even when you know each other well.

Friend: Isn't that the truth. But what makes them less than strange?

Director: A settled character, which usually happens well past youth.

Friend: What settles a character?

Director: Convictions coupled with circumstance.

Friend: Convictions alone can't settle a character?

Director: No. And neither can circumstance alone. But when combined? It's often gold.

Friend: I've never heard you say that before.

Director: We've never talked about it before.

Friend: Well, I don't know if I think it's true.

Director: Then think about it some and tell me what you conclude.

Friend: I will. But is a settled character passive?

Director: I somehow knew you'd ask. Not if your character allows you to think. Or better, not if your character prioritizes thought.

Friend: How many characters prioritize thought?

Director: There are a few, the best of which is that of a philosopher.

Friend: Tell me about the other few.

Director: They have responsibilities that pull them away from philosophy.

Friend: Do you think that's bad?

Director: It is what it is. And no, I don't think it's bad. These responsibilities need tending by someone, and who better than someone who would otherwise philosophize?

Friend: But they philosophize when they can?

Director: Certainly. And they bring much wisdom born of experience to the task.

Friend: I think I'm one of these, not a philosopher proper. But I'm not sure I bring much wisdom.

Director: Let others be the judge of that. For my part, I think you do. But wisdom must be tested in fire to prove that it's true.

Friend: What kind of fire?

Director: Discourse.

Friend: Talking isn't fire.

Director: Maybe you haven't been talking to the right people.

Friend: Are you 'right people'?

Director: There's only one way to find out. But really, Friend, haven't we kept up the flame tonight?

Friend: That's really all the test of discourse is? Friendly conversation?

Director: Friendly, yes. It's hard to learn anything otherwise. Our guard is too often up.

Friend: What part of my wisdom are we proving true or untrue?

Director: In this discourse the wisdom in question is ours, not yours alone. We share.

Friend: That's fine. But how do I test what's mine? You said to let others judge.

Director: That was an indiscretion. You go home and question yourself.

Friend: A dialogue with myself.

Director: Yes, precisely that. And then you go off with the right people and dialogue with them. And then you go home with what you learn and start all over again.

Friend: This is what you do?

Director: This is what I do.

Friend: Why did you say you made an indiscretion?

Director: Because I spoke too freely of others.

Friend: That word, 'other', has some sort of special meaning to you, doesn't it?

Director: There are those who fit neatly into categories. And then there are others.

Friend: Are you an other?

Director: I'm not sure. I may fit neatly into the category 'philosopher'.

Friend: You don't want to?

Director: It's tempting, I'll admit. But I'm really not sure.

Friend: Categories are the little prisons that dominate our lives.

Director: Well said. But do you think they're necessary?

Friend: Without categories we'd have no words.

Director: And you doubted your wisdom. That's very profound.

Friend: Thank you. But it doesn't sound so profound if we substitute a word.

Director: What word?

Friend: 'Stereotypes' for 'categories'.

Director: Stereotypes as little prisons, sure. But can we say without stereotypes we'd have no words?

Friend: No, that doesn't sound right.

Director: Do you know how I'd damn stereotypes?

Friend: Tell me.

Director: They're the height of passivity. Instead of investigating each case before us, we lump them all together and give them some name.

Friend: That's true. We pick some superficial trait and assume it gets at something profound.

Director: Something essential, yes. But stereotypes never stand up to analysis, or at least not usually.

Friend: Yes. But what does that say about analysis?

Director: It says not many analyze things.

Friend: That's very sad and true. That's the great passivity in the land.

Director: How can we spur people to think?

Friend: Show them they're wrong in each individual case.

Director: They won't believe us.

Friend: But we'll show them.

Director: People who don't want to see are as good as blind. And you can't teach the blind to see.

Friend: There has to be a way.

Director: That's the optimist in you.

Friend: So what can we do?

Director: Focus on those who want to see.

Friend: Why does one person want to see and another doesn't?

Director: Why are the stars in the sky and not at the bottom of the sea?

Friend: Because stars are bigger than our entire planet.

Director: We didn't always know that, you know.

Friend: But we know it now.

Director: Do you know it?

Friend: What do you mean?

Director: Do you know it?

Friend: Of course I know it!

Director: How do you know it? Have you been to the stars?

Friend: Of course not. But we have telescopes that show them, and give us a sense of their size.

Director: You take this on trust.

Friend: Director, you're starting to sound a little crazy.

Director: I'm just trying to say something about trust. You trust the astronomers who tell us about the stars.

Friend: Of course.

Director: Why?

Friend: Because they've proven themselves beyond a reasonable doubt.

Director: Well, the people who don't want to see have unreasonable doubts. And they're as good as blind when it comes to the stars.

Friend: But why do they doubt?

Director: Doubt against proof is a sign of belief.

Friend: What does that mean?

Director: It can mean several things. For one, it can mean you trust your instincts against 'proof'. You feel you need more time to digest this proof, and see where it's weak.

Friend: What else can it mean?

Director: It can mean that you feel belief is more important than proof.

Friend: That's only to say much the same thing.

Director: Well, then I've said it all. Do you ever believe against proof?

Friend: I'm not sure I do. Do you?

Director: No. But I have a rather high standard for proof.

Friend: But that's the thing. Some people have impossibly high standards. And yet they believe the strangest things without the merest sort of proof!

Director: No doubt it's odd. And it happens all the time. They demand an active proof while they passively accept what they will.

Friend: They're hypocritical.

Director: Maybe. But I think of them as inconsistent. What's the greater sin?

Friend: Hypocrisy, of course. Inconsistency can be inadvertent.

Director: And hypocrisy can't?

Friend: How can hypocrisy be inadvertent? Hypocrites are always to blame! But let's not argue this now. That's not what we're here for.

Director: What are we here for?

Friend: We're here to discuss passivity.

46

Director: Is the inadvertent passive?

Friend: I'd say it's accidental.

Director: Is the accidental passive?

Friend: Allowing the accidental to rule your life is. But the accidental itself is neither passive nor active.

Director: So luck itself is neither active nor passive.

Friend: True. What we do with it is.

Director: We can be active or passive in accepting or rejecting luck.

Friend: Rejecting can only be active. And I'm not sure accepting is anything but passive.

Director: We've come a long way. Remember what we said about accepting awards? But I don't know. Think of it like surfing. You actively accept the luck of the wave and ride it in.

Friend: There's skill in accepting luck?

Director: Of course there is! Luck is only the start. The rest is up to you. But do you know what else our metaphor suggests?

Friend: Tell me.

Director: Rejecting luck, a wave, is passive. You just sit there on your board and let the wave roll by.

Friend: Well, that metaphor is misleading because it often takes effort to reject bad luck.

Director: Okay. But the point is that it's not a simple thing.

Friend: Agreed.

Director: But what is simple is that we need to know good or bad luck when we see it.

Friend: That's not always easy. Something can look good and be bad, or look bad and be good.

Director: I have a proposal, but I'm not sure you'll like it.

Friend: Try me.

Director: I propose that anything that looks good, is good. And anything that looks bad, is bad. The rest depends on us. So if something looks good and turns out bad, it's our fault for not using it well. It's the same with the bad turning good. We worked some impossible miracle here.

Friend: I don't like that one bit. Appearances can deceive. You know that. There's often a difference between the superficial and the essential. And the essential takes time to know.

Director: But what if the superficial is the essential? The wave is big; the wave is small.

Friend: Yes, but when we're talking about people it's not so simple.

Director: People are luck?

Friend: Don't act surprised. You know full well that when people come into your life they bring luck.

Director: And you bring luck to them.

Friend: Of course.

Director: Do the lucks always match? If someone comes into my life as good luck, can I be bad luck to them, or do I have to be good luck, too?

Friend: It would be nice if they matched. But I'm not sure they always do.

Director: It would be nice if bad luck and bad luck met?

Friend: Yes, because it would drive them apart more quickly.

Director: What if someone is luck neutral?

Friend: I don't see how that's possible. We all bring some luck with us. It can't be helped.

Director: Can't it? I don't know. I think it's possible.

Friend: How?

Director: By being active when the other is passive, and passive when the other is active.

Friend: What does that accomplish?

Director: It cancels the luck either way.

Friend: That makes no sense.

Director: Doesn't it? I don't know. I can't help feeling there's something here. I'll have to give it more thought.

Friend: Our dialogue made you think?

Director: Yes, certainly.

Friend: Well, I'm not giving this luck-neutral stuff anymore thought. Does that make me passive?

Director: No, you just might have too many other things to think about.

Friend: That's true, and I do. Not everything is food for thought for everyone. We all have different tastes.

Director: You put that very well. And I agree, mostly.

Friend: Mostly?

Director: I sometimes wonder if there's a universal food that's to the taste of all.

Friend: What could such a thought be?

Director: Something we all have an interest in.

Friend: But interests vary so widely.

Director: Maybe something about the future of humanity?

Friend: Even there, opinions are mixed.

Director: Yes, but opinions suggest interest. And if there's interest, there might be thought.

Friend: No, opinions might suggest interest—but interest often stifles thought.

Director: We have to think against our interests?

Friend: No, I'm not saying that. We should think with our interests. Haven't we touched on this before?

Director: I think we have. But not in this light. Why think in alignment with interest?

Friend: Because interest spurs us on.

Director: But interests can be blinders.

Friend: That's okay. We can't see everything at once.

Director: Once more you're proving your wisdom. What you say is true. But don't we have to look around?

Friend: That's what active friends are for. They know when we can afford to be distracted. And we trust them and turn our gaze.

Director: A look takes trust?

Friend: Of course. There are so many things to look at. We simply cannot waste our time. But if something is recommended by a friend, it's at least worth a peek, and maybe more.

Director: Is 'maybe more' a thorough exam?

Friend: It can be, depending.

Director: Depending on what?

Friend: It our interest is truly piqued.

Director: Is it safe to say that if we don't examine something closely, we're not interested?

Friend: Of course. That's only common sense.

Director: Yes, but I have my doubts. Isn't it possible not to know our interest? And if we don't, we might leave interesting things untouched.

Friend: Well, that's a big question. I'm inclined to think we know it but don't act on it.

Director: Why wouldn't we?

Friend: We might be afraid.

Director: Afraid of our own interest?

Friend: Maybe it's more like this. People might not like our interest, and we're afraid how they'll react if we pursue it.

Director: Yes, I think you're on to something there. But shouldn't we pursue it nonetheless?

Friend: We should, but many don't.

Director: All because of fear?

Friend: And laziness. Pursuit of your interest takes work.

Director: Laziness-and-fear, that passive combination. So what can we do if we see a friend succumb to this?

Friend: We have to be careful. Friendships have ended over differences here. We have to encourage them. I think that's all we can do.

Director: And what about the opposite? Overwork-and-foolhardiness? Discourage our friend from this?

Friend: Of course. We're looking for the mean—work-and-courage. That's how you secure your interest.

Director: So courage-and-laziness gets you nowhere.

Friend: As does cowardice-and-work.

47

Director: But all of this assumes we know our interest. What good is courage-and-work if we don't?

Friend: No good.

Director: Are there many with courage-and-work who don't know?

Friend: Like I said, I'm inclined to think we know.

Director: How do we know?

Friend: We learn from experience.

Director: So there was a time before we knew, before the experience.

Friend: I suppose that's true.

Director: What if we don't have the right experiences?

Friend: All experiences are right. They all help point us to our interest.

Director: I'm not so sure about that. But what about the opposite?

Friend: What opposite?

Director: The lack of experience. What if, for instance, we never experience love? That's possible, isn't it?

Friend: Maybe. And I take your point. There may be certain experiences we're lacking, experiences that would help us on our way.

Director: How do we know we're lacking an experience?

Friend: I'm not sure we do.

Director: Maybe a friend could point this out to us, gently?

Friend: True, that might help.

Director: Then we think that thought and it helps us on our way.

Friend: Don't tell me you think thoughts are experiences.

Director: Of course they are. If you think something new you change. And change is definitely an experience. But so is the thought. And is that so strange? We have to think if we hope to know our interests.

Friend: No, I guess that's not so strange. But people are afraid of change.

Director: Even change for the better?

Friend: They don't know it's for the better. Are you going to tell me every change that's born of thought is for the better?

Director: Of course I am. So how do we persuade them?

Friend: We have to give them a taste of thought.

Director: But let's be sure. Are we saying some people never think?

Friend: That's a hard thing to say. We all think that we all think.

Director: So there are two senses of 'think'. One is our sense, the active thing. The other means something like 'to believe'. 'We all believe that we all think.' That's really what you mean, right?

Friend: Right.

Director: So if we say, "Some people never think,' we're either saying some people are never active or some people never believe.

Friend: I think we can find examples of both cases, though we should drop the 'never'.

Director: Now I wonder about this. Those who don't believe, are they necessarily active in thought? Or are they something else?

Friend: I think if you don't believe you have to think. That's how you occupy your mind.

Director: To be sure, when we say 'don't believe' we mean it in a fundamental way. You don't believe, for instance, that car ahead of you will stop at the red light. You suspect it will, you expect it will—but you don't believe.

Friend: I don't see the point in that, Director. Expecting and believing are much the same thing.

Director: I expect the sun will rise tomorrow. I believe the sun will rise tomorrow. Much the same thing, yes. So are we saying no one can get by with no belief?

Friend: We are.

Director: Then maybe the important point is this. We have to know when we believe. We have to know we don't know.

Friend: If we don't know the sun will rise, we don't know anything.

Director: So expectation, belief, and knowledge are one?

Friend: No, but there's overlap and there are questions of degree.

Director: Is the sunrise the highest degree of knowledge we can obtain?

Friend: Yes.

Director: I think there's something more certain than that.

Friend: What?

Director: That there will always be love.

Friend: I'm not as sure about that as you are. What if we live in very degenerate times?

Director: Love will find a way.

Friend: I never thought of you as a romantic.

Director: I'm not. I'm a realist here. We can count on love more than the sun. I like to think I have knowledge of this.

Friend: Why is love so special? Why more certain than the sun?

Director: As far as we know, as long as there have been humans there has been love.

Friend: We don't know that. The earliest humans may or may not have had love. There's no evidence one way or the other.

Director: And there's no evidence one way or the other that human beings as we know them will one day cease to exist. But we know the sun will burn itself out.

Friend: That's a theory. We don't actually know the sun will burn out.

Director: It's looking more like a fact every day. But no one seriously says love is going away. Or do you know of someone who does?

Friend: I don't. So what does this mean?

Director: Maybe the only thing we can know, truly know, is love.

Friend: But love is so, so... problematic!

Director: Knowledge is problematic, too. They make a good pair. But listen to us! Nothing is simpler than love. We all know love when we feel it.

Friend: But there are degrees of love. Puppy love, head over heels, obsession.

Director: I'm inclined to think love is or it isn't. And the way we feel it has to do with where we are at the time.

Friend: What do you mean, 'where we are'?

Director: How much we've thought and know about love. Or don't you think our state of mind affects how we feel?

Friend: Of course it does. But you can't think your way out of love.

Director: You can't think your way into it, either. But that doesn't mean thought has no role in love.

Friend: What is its role?

Director: It's one thing to love. It's another thing to know what to do about love.

Friend: What to say, how to act?

Director: Yes. Don't you think we need to think about these things?

Friend: No doubt we do. But it's hard to think when you're in love.

Director: If that's true, isn't it all the more reason to try?

48

Friend: So how do we think when we're in love?

Director: One way is to try and look at your situation from the outside, to see it objectively.

Friend: That never works.

Director: Another way is to stay completely inside.

Friend: What does that mean?

Director: To never leave the cave of love.

Friend: Cave?

Director: Think of it as the world of love.

Friend: So why never leave?

Director: Because if you hope to thrive, you need to take your bearings mostly from within.

Friend: Why?

Director: Because when you're in love, the outside world makes no sense, as you suggested when you said, 'That never works.'

Friend: The bearings you take while inside, they make no sense on the outside?

Director: Very little to none. That's why people just shrug at the course a lover takes. It makes no sense to them, but they somehow understand.

Friend: That makes sense. They've experienced love and know there's nothing to be done. Love must take its course.

Director: Yes. So where is thought in this? Is it in taking the bearings? Is it in thinking what to do and say?

Friend: Isn't it in all of those things?

Director: Yes, but what's important here is memory.

Friend: I don't understand.

Director: We have to remember what it was like outside while we're inside, just as those on the outside remember when they were inside and this makes them shrug and smile.

Friend: Why remember? Why not forget? Why not give ourselves completely over to love?

Director: Because if you ever fall out of love you're lost.

Friend: Many people would say they have no intention of falling out of love.

Director: Intent plays no role with love. Memory of the outside gives the mind the leverage it needs to think.

Friend: We need leverage in order to think?

Director: Yes. Do you know what a lever is?

Friend: Of course I do.

Director: It helps you move heavy or firmly fixed loads.

Friend: Move them where?

Director: Up.

Friend: Up?

Director: Love wants us to rise.

Friend: To float?

Director: In your experience, is that what happens?

Friend: In my experience, keeping things light and flexible is best. But memory of the outside can really help us here?

Director: If there's help to be had, it's from this. We gain perspective as we think with our memories in mind. But the memories also affect the direction of our thoughts. We think in ways we wouldn't without the outside in mind.

Friend: Still, people will say it's best to give yourself over to love.

Director: Why do you think they say that?

Friend: They believe in the power of love.

Director: Love has power, no doubt. All the more reason to be wary it doesn't overpower us!

Friend: What would that mean?

Director: We lose our ability to be reasonable.

Friend: Some would say that's good. What is 'being reasonable', after all? It might mean being wishy washy.

Director: I should have said we lose our power to reason. Love is a symphony that drowns out the quiet voice.

Friend: I like that. But why does reason have to be a quiet voice? Why can't it join the orchestra or sing?

Director: Reason is often shy.

Friend: It shouldn't be—especially when in love.

Director: Why especially?

Friend: We think better when in love. Love makes everything clear.

Director: I thought we said it's hard to think when in love.

Friend: Hard doesn't mean bad.

Director: True. But isn't there one important stipulation?

Friend: What?

Director: The love is returned.

Friend: You think I'll disagree? I'll take it further with another requirement, one more difficult to meet. The love must be equal on both sides.

Director: Close enough to be considered equal? Or truly equal?

Friend: Truly equal.

Director: What does equal mean?

Friend: The same. You love each other the same.

Director: And this is common?

Friend: Ha! It's rare, very rare.

Director: So thinking better when in love is rare. From the outside, how can we tell if someone is thinking better?

Friend: You'll know them by their works.

Director: So if a lover writes beautiful symphonies while in love, we know the love is equal?

Friend: Yes, assuming the works weren't as good before.

Director: We need to see a marked improvement.

Friend: Correct.

Director: Or maybe the lover only starts writing symphonies while in love, and they're good.

Friend: Yes, that tells us much.

Director: Then true love makes us more active.

Friend: It certainly does.

Director: But if it isn't true love it might make us more passive, because we don't think as well as we otherwise might.

Friend: That follows from what we're saying.

Director: So we must push away all love except the true.

Friend: Of course. Easy to say, hard to do.

Director: Why is it hard?

Friend: Love has a power over us and many give in even though the love isn't right.

Director: We want to be in love no matter the quality of that love?

Friend: Yes. That's the great temptation.

Director: Is love so good that even bad love is desired?

Friend: Yes. Love is powerful stuff.

Director: How can we learn to resist until we know it's right?

Friend: Unfortunately, we have to learn from our mistakes.

Director: And the more we learn the more we resist?

Friend: Don't you think that's how it works?

Director: I don't know. I mean, the more we know the more we can dare.

Friend: No, that's crazy. Thinking like that will only land you in trouble.

Director: Well, I don't want that. But shouldn't we be bold in love? Isn't that how we win our love?

Friend: Sometimes that's what it takes, true.

Director: Then sometimes we must dare.

Friend: But tell that to a novice and they'll dare right away.

Director: A good way to learn.

Friend: If the consequences aren't too bad. Bad love can scar you for life, you know.

Director: Some people are attracted to scars. Scars might serve you well.

Friend: You really want to defend daring in love, don't you?

Director: It doesn't need my defense. It does quite well on its own. But I wonder. Is it more active to be daring than not?

Friend: We can dare without a thought in the world.

Director: Passive daring. A very strange thing.

Friend: Why do you think it's strange? With love it happens all the time.

Director: And sometimes with success?

Friend: Sometimes, sure.

Director: Love is dependent on luck?

Friend: No, I'd say it's love dependent on a strong feeling.

Director: Can you feel that your love is equal?

Friend: I think you can feel it, yes.

Director: Then what need for thought?

Friend: Maybe you think once you're in love's cave.

Director: No thinking without but thinking within?

Friend: Oh, you think without—just not about love.

Director: Just not about such an important thing.

Friend: What can I say? Love takes us passive and makes us active in this.

Director: If love has that power, more power to love!

Friend: Do you believe it does?

Director: I've never had fully reciprocated love. Have you?

Friend: Fully? Honestly? No.

Director: Then who are we to say what wonders love can work?

Friend: That's a fair point.

Director: And we shouldn't take the risk.

Friend: What do you mean?

Director: Lying passively as we hope love will come and sweep us away.

Friend: Of course we shouldn't do that.

Director: But based on our reasoning, so many will.

Friend: More fool them.

Director: Yes. We should be active concerning love, I say. We should reason about love with potential beloveds.

Friend: And the reasoning might win their love?

Director: Not 'might', 'should'.

Friend: I agree. Is that what you've been doing all these years?

Director: It is.

Friend: With no success.

Director: I've had limited success. And you?

Friend: I'll admit it. I've been on the passive side here. But now I see the error of my ways. And even if I don't win love, I'll be doing the most important thing.

Director: That's all we can do. We have to arrange our lives around the most important thing. To do otherwise is the height of foolishness.

Friend: I agree.

49

Director: Did you see that? Those two planes almost collided!

Friend: The air traffic controller must have been asleep!

Director: I wonder why the computer didn't catch the error.

Friend: Because humans made the computer. We rely too much on computers. They're making us more and more passive as we let them run our lives.

Director: We actively make them in order to passively use them?

Friend: Yes.

Director: But surely computers can help us think. They show us things we couldn't otherwise see.

Friend: That may be. And I suppose they can do the drudge work so we can focus on higher things.

Director: How many focus on higher things? And am I right that 'higher things' means things requiring thought?

Friend: Yes, thought. And not many.

Director: When people think, what do they think about?

Friend: Mostly? Human things. Interpersonal things.

Director: Like our sex lives?

Friend: I've always hated that phrase.

Director: Why?

Friend: For a couple of reasons. One, it makes it sound like sex is a separate life from our other lives.

Director: What's the next reason?

Friend: 'Romantic life' is a better phrase than 'sex life'.

Director: Less graphic?

Friend: Yes, but that's not the main reason. It better reflects what that 'life' is.

Director: And you'd rather the romantic weren't separated from the rest of life.

Friend: Exactly.

Director: Do you give much thought to your romantic life?

Friend: I give it enough thought, I suppose.

Director: What are some of your thoughts?

Friend: That's rather personal, don't you think?

Director: Yes, but there's a problem here.

Friend: Because I won't share?

Director: That's just a symptom of a larger problem, one concerning the private. It's all too easy to be passive here.

Friend: Why?

Director: Because no one checks up on whether you think while you're there.

Friend: That's why people see psychologists.

Director: Do you?

Friend: No. Do you?

Director: No. But I think we've forgotten something. A lover checks up on what you think.

Friend: Of course. And we check up on them.

Director: Lovers encourage the active in their love.

Friend: Lovers want their lovers to think.

Director: Because they want their love to be the best it can be. When is sex good?

Friend: Excuse me?

Director: We're grown men. We can talk about these things. When is sex good?

Friend: When is it good for you?

Director: When thinking is involved.

Friend: You don't really mean that.

Director: Why not?

Friend: It doesn't work that way.

Director: It doesn't work when you think?

Friend: You have to get out of your head.

Director: Where do you go?

Friend: You know full well where you go.

Director: Well, I stay in my head.

Friend: Has that been satisfactory to you?

Director: Satisfactory? No, much better than that.

Friend: Alright, no need to brag.

Director: Who's bragging? I'm making a point.

Friend: What point?

Director: Active sex is best.

Friend: Can there be such a thing as passive sex?

Director: Yes. And it's no good.

Friend: Thoughtless sex.

Director: Drunken sex.

Friend: Sex without a point.

Director: That's the thing. There has to be a point. Otherwise sex is merely refreshing, like going for a swim.

Friend: What's wrong with going for a swim?

Director: Nothing, really. But people expect so much more from sex.

Friend: True. And there's another point. Drunken swimmers often drown.

Director: Yes, there's that. What's the point for you?

Friend: Sex reinforces love.

Director: That's a good point. If there's thought in the love, will there be thought in the sex?

Friend: Director, I'm not sure we should insist on thought everywhere. Do you think when you swim?

Director: I do.

Friend: Well, you're the exception.

Director: I think lots of people think when they swim, or run, or walk, or hike.

Friend: Well, they shouldn't think when they make love. They should take a break.

Director: That sounds like good advice.

Friend: It really is.

50

Director: So we should always think, except when we shouldn't. And we shouldn't when we're performing an act that supports one of the most important things in our lives.

Friend: You're trying to make it sound bad.

Director: No. I'm just trying to make it sound like it is. And I have your assurance that this is how it is.

Friend: You think too much.

Director: I should be more passive?

Friend: We need to re-examine whether thinking is the ultimate activity.

Director: Alright. What's more active than thought? Triathlons?

Friend: Of course not.

Director: Making money?

Friend: What? What are you talking about?

Director: So many of us dedicate ourselves to making money. It would be a shame if this is no active thing at all.

Friend: It's active, but not the ultimate in activity.

Director: How about thoughtless sex? A great activity? The highest?

Friend: No.

Director: Then what?

Friend: I... don't know.

Director: Then we need to think. Thinking might see us through.

Friend: I like that you say it 'might'.

Director: Because it shows I'm not dogmatic?

Friend: Yes. Thinking might not be all it's said to be.

Director: I can go along with that. But how would we know?

Friend: You want me to say we know through thought.

Director: Well, that's how I think we know. Is there another way?

Friend: We can see with our own two eyes.

Director: And then in order to register what we see we must give it thought, if only for an instant. Haven't you heard of people 'seeing' but not taking in what they see?

Friend: I have. Some people believe what they're told more than they believe what they see.

Director: They don't know what to think unless someone tells them what they saw.

Friend: Exactly. But they're not really thinking. They're.... They're.... What are they doing?

Director: Formulating opinions based on others' words.

Friend: Yes, that's what they're doing. Why do you think they do this?

Director: This is one of the most passive things of all. And why do they do it? Laziness and fear.

Friend: Too lazy to think for themselves? Afraid of what others might think of their independently formed opinions? I think that's right.

Director: But there's something more. There's a strong desire to belong.

Friend: Yes! I think you hit it on the head. Shared opinions make for social glue.

Director: Because nearly everyone wants to belong somewhere in some way.

Friend: You can belong and still be independent.

Director: I don't doubt that's possible. But how many are?

Friend: Not many. There are so many followers.

Director: Is it bad to be a follower?

Friend: Why do you even ask?

Director: Well, is it good to be a leader?

Friend: Of course it is.

Director: If it's bad to be a follower, it's bad to be a leader.

Friend: Why do you say that?

Director: The best leaders know how to follow. That way they know what to expect from those they lead.

Friend: You can know how and never do it.

Director: Then how would you know how?

Friend: You think your way through.

Director: Some things you have to experience for yourself.

Friend: Are you placing experience above thought?

Director: Experience is food for thought. And if you want to be a leader, you need to eat the follower food.

Friend: Does thought always need food?

Director: It starves if it doesn't have it.

Friend: What kind of thought does a starving mind produce?

Director: Distorted thought. Sickly thought. Thought that won't stand up.

Friend: Is experience the only food? Can't a good book be food for thought?

Director: It can. But it's the experience of reading—living with that book—that makes for food.

Friend: What do you mean by living with a book?

Director: You don't just read it. Any idiot can read a book. But it takes someone special to savor the book, to take it to heart, to make something of it—to make the book a part of their life.

Friend: I take your point. I have a few books like this. But do you expect we have many?

Director: Some people only have one. But that's not enough for perspective. Some people have hundreds. But that's too dilute. You need a good number here.

Friend: What's a good number?

Director: Oh, it all depends. But if I had to say? Twenty seems like a good number to me.

Friend: Twenty books to live by. And I take it you have to read them more than once?

Director: In a year I'd read all twenty through. And then the next year. And then the next year. Of course, I'd still have to read more broadly than that.

Friend: But you keep on coming back to the twenty.

Director: Yes. You always keep on coming back. And for some people the cycle is longer. Every three years, let's say. Or ten.

Friend: Some people are slow readers.

Director: Some of the best, indeed. There's a danger for those who read very quickly. They might think they understand when they don't.

Friend: And then they act on that false understanding.

Director: Yes they do.

Friend: Tell me, Director. Is dwelling with books an active thing?

Director: You're in constant dialogue with the books, so yes.

Friend: But don't some people dwell with no thought?

Director: That's the temptation here.

Friend: The books give us a ready-made world.

Director: They can.

Friend: And we exercise our imagination, which is different than thought, to tailor that world to our needs.

Director: You put that very well. We should question these books, not inflate them with imagination. We ask them serious questions, and if they're truly good books, they answer.

Friend: But the answers aren't always obvious, are they?

Director: To hard questions there are no good and obvious answers. We wrestle with these books and seek to have them tell us what they know.

Friend: Is that how you deal with people? You wrestle with them and seek to have them tell you what they know?

Director: I do.

Friend: Are you wrestling with me tonight?

Director: Just as you've been wrestling with me.

Friend: A friendly wrestling match can do us some good.

Director: And more than some if we're lucky.

51

Friend: How does luck figure into it? Wrestling is a matter of skill.

Director: Yes but the best matches are when the wrestlers are evenly paired. They test one another that way. Otherwise there's a risk someone will get away with absurdities.

Friend: I take your point. I think there's also a risk that someone will only wrestle with half a mind.

Director: When we wrestle we must try with all our might. Otherwise there is no point.

Friend: Agreed. So it takes luck for a good partner and then a willingness to try. Then we're fully active.

Director: And when we go away we must think about the match.

Friend: The match is experience.

Director: Yes, exactly so.

Friend: But do you really try with all your might against someone who isn't evenly paired?

Director: Yes, but here the wrestling metaphor must end. I try with all my might with, not against, such a person. We help each other see.

Friend: I thought we need to see on our own. You need someone to tell you what to see?

Director: See with the eyes and you don't need someone to say what you saw. But seeing with the mind is a different thing. Here we can often use some help.

Friend: So you're saying you need someone to tell you what to think?

Director: No, I'm saying sometimes others can help us clear things up. For instance, suppose I think all snakes are dangerous. But then I find myself in conversation with a lover of snakes, who tells me it simply isn't true. Not all snakes are dangerous. I'll want to verify, but this helps clear up my mind about snakes.

Friend: I see what you mean. Is every time you clear your mind an active thing?

Director: Clearing is thinking, so based on what we've been saying the answer is yes.

Friend: I think that's important. I was having a hard time understanding what thinking is. But making things clear... clears it up!

Director: Yes, but there's a temptation here. Some people make things appear more simple than they are. In doing this, they seem to clear things up. But in the end, they only make things more complicated than they need to be.

Friend: How do they make things more complex if they simplify?

Director: Suppose the topic they discuss consists of A and B. They say it's all answered by C. No need for A and B. So much less work.

Friend: But you said they complexify.

Director: And they do—for those who wish to know the truth. Now the truth lovers have to look into and get clear on both A, B, and C. By my math, that's fifty percent more work than A and B alone.

Friend: Assuming C doesn't solve A and B.

Director: That's our assumption, Friend—though we're open to being wrong.

Friend: I think a lot of influential people argue for the A-and-B-answering C.

Director: You'll find it nearly everywhere you look.

Friend: Because people would rather believe one thing than think about two?

Director: That's how it seems to me.

Friend: But how hard is it to think about two?

Director: It's not so bad. But those who promote a C let on that it's much more than A and B in play. They suggest there's so much more, the whole alphabet in fact. They strongly advise it's best to stick with C. And those who are easily frightened agree.

Friend: I knew there was fear mongering here. These people want everyone to passively believe in C. But do they, the fear mongers, actively think themselves?

Director: What would they think?

Friend: Didn't they have to come up with some sort of synthesis of A and B? Didn't that take thought?

Director: What's to think? They just make something up and see if it sticks. Eventually they have success. Is that so hard?

Friend: I guess it's not. But it's important for their followers to believe they, their leaders, have thought it all through. Isn't it?

Director: I think it is. Even in the depraved depths of mental passivity, the idea of thought has value.

Friend: But the wantonly passive need to think they've thought. Don't they?

Director: I don't know. I think they can think they're smart enough to know the truth when they hear it. That makes them seem better than many who are lost in the A and B.

Friend: How do you wrestle with someone who believes in C?

Director: You have to keep on bringing up A and B.

Friend: But they're not going to want to hear it.

Director: No doubt. But you have to persist.

Friend: They'll get angry at you.

Director: They likely will. So you have to decide if it's worth it to you to carry on.

Friend: When would you carry on?

Director: When there's a chance they might turn to the facts.

Friend: How can you tell?

Director: It takes practice. But basically you look for an opening.

Friend: What sort of opening?

Director: A chink in their armor.

Friend: But what sort of chink?

Director: It could be anything. A fond memory of A. A secret longing for B. You just have to look and see.

Friend: And then you exploit what you see?

Director: 'Exploit' sounds so negative. I would say I encourage them to further explore the A or B.

Friend: So you're really only getting them to do what they already want.

Director: Yes.

Friend: And what about C?

Director: I tell them to forget it.

Friend: And if they can't?

Director: Maybe they make it their life's work to refute the C.

Friend: You don't really mean that.

Director: Why wouldn't I?

Friend: Isn't that a waste of time?

Director: I think they might derive satisfaction from it. And it might help others return to A and B. What's wrong with that?

Friend: Is dedicating yourself to refuting nonsense active? I mean, what if you just use the same old arguments each time? You're not really thinking, are you?

Director: You have a point. That's why when they're done with arguing against C they think about A and B, and maybe even D and E. There's a whole great big alphabet out there, Friend, all of it ripe for thinking.

Friend: And if we master the alphabet?

Director: You can always learn another language with another alphabet. There's really no shortage here.

Friend: What does 'language' mean?

Director: I'd describe it as a system of thought.

Friend: Why would you want to learn a system of thought?

Director: I would want to learn it so I could interact with the native speakers.

Friend: And get them to reject their C's in favor of exotic A's and B's?

Director: Something like that. Again, what's wrong with that?

Friend: Nothing. I admit I'm intrigued. But languages don't come that easily to me.

Director: Find a toehold wherever you can and see if you can't climb. And don't bother about those who are faster. It's your adventure you're on, not theirs. They have their own problems, problems that come with speed.

Friend: What kind of problems?

Director: Sometimes they outpace the natives and can't communicate well. Sometimes they go too far and can't find their way back. Things like this.

Friend: Better to be slow and steady?

Director: When you're slow and steady? Yes, it is. It's best to be what you are.

Friend: Can we be other than we are?

Director: I think we can. We forget ourselves.

Friend: But that forgetting usually involves trying to do more than we can.

Director: Yes, but not always. Some of us forget to try to do what we know we can do.

Friend: Why would we forget?

Director: The power of inertia, fear, shame.

Friend: Shame? What do you mean? Why be ashamed of doing what you can do?

Director: What is shame?

Friend: Consciousness of wrong or foolish behavior.

Director: Yes, but there's a bit missing. You suffer something because of your behavior.

Friend: Of course.

Director: Suppose we know we can upstage our boss, and not in a bad way; in a way that can be to the good of all involved. But we don't do it because we'd be ashamed to upstage anyone in any way.

Friend: We were raised properly, taught never to do this.

Director: We believe upstaging is always wrong. So we forget that this is a real possibility for us. Do you want to know why we believe it's wrong?

Friend: I do.

Director: I see two reasons. One, we don't want to blemish our character with such behavior. Two, we make a prudential calculation and our math says we'll end up with the short end of the stick if we try to upstage.

Friend: Which of those possibilities would you try to work with?

Director: Which would you?

Friend: The character one.

Director: Why?

Friend: Because we can teach them that upstaging, when done right, is no blemish. And you?

Director: I would work on the math. We'd explore if failing to upstage actually gets you the short end of the stick. In certain cases it does, you know.

Friend: Sometimes you just have to step forward. But knowing when and how is hard!

Director: That's why you have to practice.

Friend: Practice upstaging? Ha, ha. That sounds bad. You'll get a reputation for that.

Director: For speaking up when it's required? Good, I'll take it. So many hang back until it's too late.

Friend: So how do you know when?

Director: I talk to everyone and get a general sense of the room. That way I know if I have backing if I move to upstage.

Friend: So you're not as bold as I had imagined.

Director: I'm bold but mostly with little boldnesses. Each person I sound for their opinions requires a bit of the bold. But then when it comes time to upstage, and I'm well prepared, only a little boldness is required, not some great boldness that many people imagine.

Friend: I think I could do this.

Director: I think you could, too.

Friend: It's a good way to stay active, soliciting opinions.

Director: Yes, you can think about all of them at home at night. Then you decide what to say the next day. And when you've said, you'll receive feedback on the thoughts you shared, for you to think about again at home that night.

Friend: And that's what you do?

Director: That's what I do.

Friend: The more you converse, the more you think?

Director: For me, yes. But there are others who are like deep wells. A word falls in and they have to examine this word in depth for quite some time before they're ready to speak. They're easily overwhelmed. Upstaging doesn't come easy to them. They often remain silent for long stretches of time. But when they're finally ready... look out.

Friend: What happens when they make their move?

Director: Something that's largely unexpected and explosive.

Friend: I bet that gives everyone in the room much food for thought.

Director: It usually does, and sometimes for years.

Friend: What then?

Director: For the one who spoke up? He or she is often in a state of shock.

Friend: They surprised themselves?

Director: Yes. It's one thing to think it all through. It's another thing to say it aloud.

Friend: Saying it aloud is the act that caps all the acts of thought that prepared the way.

Director: Well put. But now, many words will be tossed into our friend's well. It will take a long time to think them all through.

Friend: So, what, our friend has to retreat?

Director: I think that's best. So maybe the upstaging should be timed right in front of a planned vacation or some other long trip away.

Friend: At the very least on a Friday afternoon.

Director: Right, the weekend can help. But you should never do it at a bar.

Friend: Why not?

Director: For one, it's noisy. And you can't be sure everyone can hear. Two, you want to be loose, but not too loose. People who store things up can sometimes go too far, and then they feel ashamed. You want to hit your mark and not go too far wide or above.

Friend: So you do this at a formal business meeting?

Director: Yes, I think that's best. You get the greatest impact that way.

Friend: But also the greatest risk.

Director: If you're prepared, things will be alright.

Friend: And if you're not, you have to resign?

Director: I was prepared. And it was worth it.

Friend: How so?

Director: The other ten people in that room now have something to think about tonight.

Friend: You threw away your career so ten people might have something to think about tonight?

Director: I wouldn't say I threw it away. I traded it in for something more important.

Friend: I have to say, Director, you practice what you preach. And what about you? Do you have new things to think about now?

Director: From our conversation, sure.

Friend: And not from the resignation?

Director: But we've been talking all about the resignation—in rather uncommon depth.

52

Friend: How did you know upstaging the boss would make him force you to quit?

Director: I know the boss. He can be a bully at times. Bullies can't stand to lose face. So when he proposed his bad idea, I stepped forward and presented the reasons why it was bad and suggested we discuss another.

Friend: You had no idea of your own.

Director: No, but I knew several of the others did.

Friend: Did they put them forward?

Director: No.

Friend: Was that a surprise?

Director: Not a surprise, though a mild disappointment.

Friend: So your resignation left you with a bitter taste?

Director: Not bitter, no. The fact that no one came forward will weigh heavily in all their thoughts.

Friend: You think they'll be ashamed.

Director: Some of them will.

Friend: Can good come from shame?

Director: Shame can force you to think, if you have the right character. And I'm certain some of these ten have the right characters.

Friend: What will come of their thoughts?

Director: I don't know. But I do know they'll want to do something to cleanse themselves of their shame.

Friend: Do you think they deserve to feel shame?

Director: No.

Friend: But they didn't speak up!

Director: There's no shame in that. They weren't ready. And there's no shame in that, either.

Friend: Then why not tell them that?

Director: I will. After they think about things. Sometimes it's best to let things cool before you revisit them.

Friend: What if they need much more time?

Director: Some might need months, years even. I have to gauge this when I see them.

Friend: What if their shame keeps them away from you?

Director: Then it will be easy to know they need more time.

Friend: Aren't you ashamed that you're using them?

Director: Using them?

Friend: As disciples of sorts.

Director: I'm not looking for followers.

Friend: What are you looking for?

Director: Friends.

Friend: But you could have followers, you know.

Director: Could I? What do followers do? What's their act?

Friend: They try to learn your ways.

Director: When what they really need to do is learn their own ways. No thank you. I'll have none.

Friend: But who will make your thought live on?

Director: Is thought not worth it if it doesn't live on?

Friend: I... never thought about that before. I thought thought was the end.

Director: Thought is the means.

Friend: The means for what?

Director: Living a wonderful life. Can you object to that?

Friend: Who would? But if you live a truly wonderful life, your life will live on.

Director: You'll be famous for having a wonderful life?

Friend: That's how it ought to be. Don't you agree?

Director: If it encourages others to live their own wonderful lives, yes. But if it fosters pointless emulation, no.

Friend: What's the difference between the two?

Director: The difference is between the active and the passive. Active minded people will learn a thing or two and then move on. Passive minded people will dwell on these things.

Friend: You make it sound like the difference is between hunters and farmers.

Director: How so?

Friend: Farmers dwell; hunters move on.

Director: Oh. But hunters can range the same old tired ground. And farmers can move on from season to season to newer and better fields. There's no set rule.

Friend: And that's what makes you active? Having no set rule?

Director: You can have rules. But you think about these rules.

Friend: Are rules likely to stand if you're always questioning them?

Director: You're worried they will become provisional rules?

Friend: Opportunistic rules, yes.

Director: What's wrong with opportunistic rules?

Friend: The very name confounds them!

Director: You don't believe we should let opportunity in when it knocks?

Friend: Let it in, sure. But don't make it your rule! No one can trust you if you do.

Director: Only those who see a similar opportunity.

Friend: Brothers in opportunity. Ha!

Director: And sisters, too. What's wrong with opportunity? Are you forgetting we're talking about opportunity to live the active life of thought?

Friend: It's so easy to forget.

Director: Why?

Friend: Because it runs counter to common sense.

Director: Because common sense doesn't see thought as an activity.

Friend: Common sense says there's thinking and then there's doing.

Director: What does your sense tell you?

Friend: That thought is the highest kind of act.

Director: So why do you care what others think?

Friend: Because I have to live with them!

Director: So do I.

Friend: But you were forced to resign! I'm sorry.

Director: Don't be sorry for saying what you really think. The job is more important than being active for you.

Friend: No! Being active is most important. But you have to know when to speak up.

Director: You only speak up when it's safe.

Friend: I'm not saying that.

Director: What are you saying? You have to speak up sooner or later or you won't have anything more to think about. Does that make sense?

Friend: It does.

Director: And we can't always know when it's safe. Sometimes we're surprised. Does that also make sense?

Friend: It makes sense.

Director: Then speak when you think best. But be prepared. And don't back down.

53

Friend: How do you prepare?

Director: You practice in other conversations.

Friend: With friends, you mean.

Director: Yes, and even passing acquaintances or even strangers on the street. The point is that there won't be any blow up. Just a pleasant chat where you can air your views and allow the other to respond.

Friend: Enough of those will prepare you for the big upstage?

Director: They can certainly help. But you have to work your way up to conversations where the stakes are higher. Maybe with your wife, for instance.

Friend: Ha! She barely talks to me as it is!

Director: Then you should cherish the opportunity. Tell her what you're thinking about. See if she doesn't already have thoughts of her own. This might open doors for you.

Friend: Or slam them in my face.

Director: However that may be, you won't know unless you try.

Friend: I'll try. But I wish you could be there to help.

Director: I'll find a date and the four of us can get together over dinner. How's that?

Friend: That sounds great. But what kind of date will you find?

Director: One with a philosophical bent.

Friend: Wonderful! Two philosophers and my wife and me!

Director: Why are you being sarcastic?

Friend: What could we possibly say to you?

Director: Why, whatever you think. And that's what we'll say to you. That's how conversations work.

Friend: Okay, okay. We'll do it. And then I'll be ready to show up the boss?

Director: Only you will know when you're ready. But don't just assume you need to show him up because I did. You have to have a reason to show him up.

Friend: What was your reason?

Director: It was my reason, and so it is still. You have to have your reason, one you keep to yourself.

Friend: I thought we discuss all things.

Director: When you outwardly 'do', as opposed to think, you need to have a reason that encourages you. This reason is the product of your thought, and your thought alone. When you're certain the reason is good, you act on it, without distractions from anyone else. After the fact, you can feel free to share the reason for what you did. But I have found that doing the outward act often extinguishes the need to share the reason.

Friend: Why?

Director: If it's a good act, it sets many things in motion.

Friend: And the reason is lost in all this?

Director: No, the reason is with you always. And maybe one day you'll share. The people and time must be right.

Friend: It's so lonely when you outwardly do.

Director: But not when you act in speech? Do you feel alone tonight?

Friend: No. But I have a lot of solitary thinking to do when I get home.

Director: We're lucky. It's not every day we can have a conversation like this, one that gives us so much food for thought.

Friend: True. But you know? I'm hungry. The food at the reception was meagre. Are you hungry? Let's stop at this great little restaurant I know. We'll still make it back in time before it all ends.

* * * * * *

PART THREE

SCENE: A RESTAURANT

54

Friend: Eating is such a passive thing.

Director: But we have to digest. Digestion is as active as it gets.

Friend: You'd compare digestion to thinking?

Director: Of course I would. Thinking breaks things down into something we can use.

Friend: And then the body uses food to build up muscle or fat.

Director: What's the fat of the mind?

Friend: Unwarranted beliefs.

Director: So if I believe I can be president one day, that's fat?

Friend: Well, maybe you can—if you don't resign.

Director: How about this? I believe I can play professional football one day.

Friend: That would be fat.

Director: Why?

Friend: Because you're too old, to say nothing of your prowess.

Director: What would be fat for you?

Friend: If I believed I could be a philosopher.

Director: Why can't you?

Friend: I compare myself to you. You've had thousands of conversations like this. I've had exactly one.

Director: Maybe I'm so thickheaded I needed that many. You might only need a few.

Friend: You really think that?

Director: Yes. But remember, only you know what you need. I can't tell you how many conversations or what sort of conversations will do the trick. It's all up to you.

Friend: That's refreshing in a way. But it's also a little scary.

Director: The exciting is always a little scary, isn't it?

Friend: Point taken. So what's the muscle of the mind? Knowledge?

Director: I think of knowledge more as the product of reasoning.

Friend: So reason is the muscle.

Director: Yes.

Friend: What is reason?

Director: I wish I had an answer.

Friend: You don't know? Why not say it's logical thinking?

Director: Because sometimes reason proceeds by leaps.

Friend: Is that... good?

Director: It can be if it gets you by hopeless tangles. But you're right to question here. Leaps are the exception and not the rule.

Friend: What if you find yourself in a land of passive tangles? Shouldn't you actively leap and leap again?

Director: In that case I'd say yes. But we can't just leap every time things get difficult. At some point we really need to think our way through.

Friend: We use logic to think our way through.

Director: Logic and analogous thinking. But that can be dangerous. No two things are truly alike.

Friend: So if we say all A's are B, that doesn't always hold.

Director: Right, because we fall for the temptation to group together all seeming A's when in fact not all of them are A.

Friend: You're more radical than I thought. But I agree. People might not understand what it is that makes an A, the characteristic thing.

Director: Yes, that's true. But we don't give up on analogous thought just because there are problems. A might be more like B than not. To ignore that fact is a mistake.

Friend: So thinking means knowing things for what they are.

Director: That's what thinking is, by whatever means. Once we know what something is, we can use logic to our heart's content. But those who use logic when they don't know? No one is as deceiving.

Friend: That's a strong statement to make.

Director: Yes, and it's true. Logic blesses unthinking thoughts often enough. And it's hard to dislodge once the blessing is in.

Friend: How do we dislodge it?

Director: Whether it's in our own minds or those of others it's much as we said. We find the chink and focus there.

Friend: That will likely annoy someone greatly.

Director: Yes, it likely will. But think of the damage done if this logic of theirs goes on to gather strength.

Friend: The stakes are high.

Director: Very high.

Friend: Lazy logic versus righteous thought.

Director: How about another word for 'righteous'?

Friend: Honest?

Director: Maybe. What else?

Friend: I don't know. What do you think?

Director: I think we just say, 'Lazy logic versus thought.'

Friend: Because lazy logic is counterfeit thought.

Director: Right. Thought should need no descriptor.

Friend: I agree. But lazy logic puts something forward to 'know'. What does thought, reason, do other than attack?

Director: The attack produces knowledge in some of the minds of those who witness it.

Friend: Why only 'some of'?

Director: Not all minds are ready for knowledge.

Friend: I thought you were going to say the knowledge might belong only to certain minds.

Director: That, too. The point is that not everyone can learn from everything all the time. But if there are some who can learn something, then it's worth the effort.

Friend: You wouldn't attack unless there were witnesses?

Director: I'd attack one-on-one if I sensed the other was ready to open up to reason. And that would be preferred.

Friend: So you'd only attack in public those who aren't open to reason, in front of witnesses, witnesses who can learn.

Director: It would do no good to attack them one-on-one.

Friend: You'd attack and expect to be repulsed?

Director: Yes, but there's much to learn in the character of the repulsion.

Friend: Much for your witnesses to learn.

Director: And I'd learn, too. It's a very good thing.

55

Friend: But can't you win and have others learn from the victory?

Director: Why expose someone to potential embarrassment when you can achieve the goal one-on-one?

Friend: So you never win in public.

Director: And not always in private, either.

Friend: This doesn't sound like it's something for me. Are there philosophers who never fight?

Director: Person-to-person? Yes, some never fight there.

Friend: Where do they fight?

Director: In books.

Friend: And if they don't at least fight in books?

Director: Without the fight, without the cause, there can be no philosophy.

Friend: It's that important?

Director: What else do you think philosophy is?

Friend: Discovering truth.

Director: The truth becomes clear through the course of the fight.

Friend: Error fighting is the source of truth?

Director: Yes, for any truth worth its name.

Friend: But so much is built upon these errors.

Director: Then it's a good thing I proceed one person at a time.

Friend: But what about books? They teach many more than one.

Director: Sure, but how many will understand?

Friend: Then why write books?

Director: For some people that's their way. What can I say?

Friend: Why don't you write books?

Director: I've done a considerable bit of writing, but books really aren't my way.

Friend: What is it about books?

Director: The temptation toward passivity.

Friend: Because you imagine you're fighting when you're really not?

Director: Yes, in a word. If I'm going to write I prefer to write letters that call for response.

Friend: Do you always get a response?

Director: No, not always.

Friend: People are such cowards.

Director: Don't be too hard. Shifting from passive to active is no easy thing. I often take it as a good thing if I get no reply.

Friend: Because they've gone off to think?

Director: That's right. That's my hope.

Friend: I thought philosophers didn't indulge in hopes.

Director: This one does.

Friend: Have your hopes been realized?

Director: I don't know.

Friend: Oh of course you know! Haven't you seen someone turn active?

Director: Yes, but the question is whether it will catch, will become a self-sustaining life. That I can't know until the end.

Friend: What do you mean?

Director: The end of life. There's always temptation to turn passive again. So I can hardly know if there was true success the whole life through.

Friend: That's a pretty high standard.

Director: The highest. And my true friends wouldn't have it any other way.

Friend: No pressure on me!

Director: But isn't that what you want? The fully active life? Can you go back to passivity now, if ever you were there before?

Friend: I've been there. And no, I don't want to go back. But I'm not perfect, Director. And I have much to learn.

Director: No one is perfect, Friend. I catch myself napping all the time. But when I do I wake myself up. That's the difference here. That's what our friends are like. They try.

Friend: Well I, for one, will try.

Director: Good. And wake me up when I'm asleep.

Friend: I'll try my best. But there's a problem here.

Director: Oh?

Friend: You, Director, can be persuasive even when you're wrong.

Director: Then get some other friends and bombard me with good sense from every side. I promise you that will make me come around.

Friend: You've got it. But first we need to make such friends.

Director: Make as in create?

Friend: What? You're talking crazy.

Director: Good. Just had to be sure you weren't talking crazy yourself.

Friend: Is this what I can expect from philosophy? Checks against talking crazy?

Director: Sometimes. But sometimes you have the highest flights of rhetoric and the most involved dialectic.

Friend: That's really not my thing.

Director: Oh it's not that hard to follow if you keep your eye on the ball.

Friend: And what's the ball?

Director: The point.

Friend: Yes, yes. But what's the point?

Director: Always ask yourself, 'What am I being asked to believe?' That's the key to all of philosophy.

Friend: I think you're right. Flim-flam artists always want us to believe.

Director: And not just them. Highly respectable people want to make us believe.

Friend: Believe in what?

Director: Usually? Something that props them up.

Friend: And money is usually involved.

Director: Money is almost always involved.

Friend: What can we do?

Director: Disabuse the supporters of their leader's beliefs. Then the money dries up.

Friend: We have to prove the beliefs are false.

Director: Yes, and especially the belief the flim-flam artist holds most dear.

Friend: What if he or she doesn't believe anything? What if it's just one great big scam?

Director: I trust my experience on this. There's always something they believe. It's not always easy to see. But there's no doubt it's there.

Friend: I wish I could be as certain as you are on this.

Director: Haven't you ever heard the saying, 'Nature abhors a vacuum'? It means something always rushes in. There can be no vacuum in a human soul. There's always something there. Find it, and you can win the fight. But be careful, because the followers won't want to believe you.

Friend: I know. They'll likely even attack. So what's the point of trying to help people like that?

Director: That's a good question. I'd spend my efforts on those who want to be helped. But saying 'helped' is a bit misleading. Because they can help us.

Friend: So we help each other. Active to active.

Director: Yes. That's the only way. If it's not two-way, something is wrong.

Friend. Everyone has to bring something to the table.

Director: That's right. It's the only way things make sense. It's not a charity.

Friend: That's refreshing to hear. Having something in it for you means it can be sustained.

Director: I call it the natural economy. It's been around for thousands of years.

Friend: Why haven't I heard about it before?

Director: Passive-to-passive is the background noise in our world. That's mostly what people hear. Active-to-passive is more rare. And—

Friend: Wait a minute. Active-to-passive? What's an example of that?

Director: A thinker panders to the passive.

Friend: With no hopes of making them active?

Director: No, none.

Friend: What does the thinker hope to get out of it?

Director: Control.

Friend: That's very sad.

Director: But the odds are that this thinker isn't thinking as much as he or she could.

Friend: They need prodding from another active.

Director: Yes. The passive won't help them here.

Friend: No one can think of everything on their own.

Director: As far as I know, it's never been done.

Friend: Why would an 'active' ever want to control the passive?

Director: All I can say is that they have somehow been arrested in their development.

Friend: Is it lust for power? Fame?

Director: For all I know it's revenge. Who can say? We should ask them.

Friend: Ha! They'd never agree to talk to us.

Director: Why not?

Friend: Because they sense that we're the real thinkers, despite their claim to the title.

Director: Philosophy suffers from problems like this. Certain 'thinkers' think they can create systems that will ultimately control the way people think.

Friend: Can they?

Director: No. The unintended is overwhelming. They might get a few graduate students, and their students, and maybe even their students, to think the way they want. But no one can control another's thought. There will be drift. And the philosophy will become unrecognizable within a few generations.

Friend: Unless there's a book.

Director: True, but the meaning of that book will become harder and harder to access as time goes on.

Friend: Then why do philosophers write?

Director: Some write because they love to write. Others write because they hope to be of some use.

Friend: You mean they hope to spur thought.

Director: Yes. And that, I think, is the most we can hope. More than that is arrogance and foolishness.

Friend: But the earliest philosophers hoped for more than that. Didn't they?

Director: They were exploring the possible. And I would say that much of what they wrote backfired on them. We don't need to learn the same lesson twice.

Friend: I can't help feeling there's something important about the fact that the written word never changes.

Director: It never changes unless there are errors, unintentional or intentional, in transmission. But by and large? What's written never changes. That's why I have the confidence to conclude that the earliest philosophers were truly philosophers and not active-to-passive charlatans.

Friend: Sophists.

Director: Right. The sophists, many of whom were largely active, taught tricks to the passive for money.

Friend: I think we have our share of sophists today.

Director: No doubt.

Friend: What can be done about them?

Director: We can steal their students.

Friend: You wouldn't try to convert a sophist to a fully active life?

Director: Sure, I'd try, depending on the sophist. But even in this, nothing gets their attention better—than taking their students away.

56

Friend: But we don't take them on as our students, do we?

Director: No, they become our equals in dialogue.

Friend: But what if they're not... equal?

Director: They listen and learn and contribute what they can. I often find myself a listener to the dialogues of others. Sometimes listening is the most active thing you can do.

Friend: Listening to the right conversations can make you think.

Director: Yes, it certainly can.

Friend: Can we advance to the point where everything makes us think?

Director: I'd rather say we can advance to the point where we can learn to think wherever we are. We make ourselves think.

Friend: Then why do we say a conversation can make us think?

Director: Sometimes we need a spark to light the flame. But if we can keep the flame going, we bring it with us wherever we are.

Friend: Is your flame always lit?

Director: No, not always. It goes out more often than I care to admit. When it does I seek inspiration, I seek a spark.

Friend: And you find it in conversation?

Director: Often times, yes.

Friend: Where else do you find it?

Director: In books.

Friend: Books are a sort of conversation in the mind.

Director: Of course they are. And if you find the right ones you'll spark.

Friend: How do you know if your flame is lit?

Director: How do you know when you're thinking? More often than not you're discovering and challenging the assumptions you make.

Friend: What happens once you discover them all?

Director: I don't know of anyone who's ever run out. As we live we constantly take in new experiences. And as a rule we form assumptions about these experiences. We need to work to root the assumptions out.

Friend: And turn them into knowledge?

Director: Yes. That's life.

Friend: But now we have two flames. Thinking and knowledge.

Director: I like to think that the two flames blend into one. But remember, these metaphors aren't meant to be exact. They're just meant to help us on our way.

Friend: Of course. Assumptions are passive, aren't they?

Director: They're easy and passive, yes. But sometimes we need to make them.

Friend: That's funny. I was just going to say that.

Director: Some people make an assumption and treat it like a fact. Others make working assumptions, assumptions they test all along the way.

Friend: And if they pass all the tests? Knowledge?

Director: Well, here's a hard truth. Most of our knowledge is working knowledge.

Friend: Why?

Director: Because we can't be certain we've tested it in every possible way.

Friend: Then we're never sure about anything? Are we back to saying we can't be sure the sun will rise?

Director: No, we can be sure. But we have to be open to questioning what we know in light of new facts. That's all.

Friend: That doesn't sound so bad.

Director: It's not, especially once you make it a habit.

Friend: But we said habit is passive.

Director: This is the one exception.

Friend: Okay. I suppose we can't expect to go through life with no habits at all.

Director: A habit can be a support. And sometimes we need support.

Friend: We need support to think.

Director: We do. But we have to be careful that our support doesn't distort our thinking.

Friend: How so?

Director: Have you ever been to one of those philosophy forums where everyone is going crazy challenging everyone else's thought?

Friend: I haven't.

Director: You can't make a single statement, not a sentence, without a dozen people pouncing on you and shredding every word.

Friend: They attack out of habit?

Director: Yes, out of principle even. There's no reasoning, no consideration, just knee-jerk attack.

Friend: And they think they're thinking.

Director: They do.

Friend: Thinking means you weigh and measure, not just throw everything out.

Director: Try and tell that to them.

Friend: What you said about principle is interesting. Principles can make for habits.

Director: They can. Do you know when they don't?

Friend: When the principle is not to be passive. The one exception.

Director: Exactly.

Friend: But that doesn't make sense. What if my principle is to be honest?

Director: Have you forgotten the Nazis already? Are you honest to them?

Friend: Okay, you have a point. You have to think, if only a little, about when to be honest or not.

Director: That little bit of thinking makes all the difference.

Friend: I think people think thinking is more than it is. They think of that statue called The Thinker. They think it has to be heavy and even painful.

Director: It can be. But it can also be light and fun.

Friend: Fun?

Director: Sure! You've never had fun thinking?

Friend: I don't think I have. How can I?

Director: Think about everyday assumptions you make, small things, and go from there.

Friend: But I want to think about serious things.

Director: You don't think everyday things are serious?

Friend: But you said they're fun!

Director: We can make the serious fun.

Friend: How?

Director: By not taking it too seriously.

Friend: But you have to take the serious seriously!

Director: Of course you do. But not too seriously. Just seriously enough.

Friend: Well, that makes sense. How do you know when it's enough?

Director: Oh, I think plenty of people will be ready to tell you.

Friend: That's true. But if they sense you're having fun they're going to get upset. So what do we do? Hide our fun? Suppress our smiles?

Director: You can try, but it will come out in your eyes.

Friend: That's very true. So what do we do?

Director: Be prepared to take a hit.

Friend: That's no fun.

Director: You just have to roll with it, Friend.

Friend: I'm not sure I like this kind of fun.

Director: Let me guess. You'd be serious for the sake of success.

Friend: Why do you bring up success?

Director: Too many hits and you likely won't have 'success'. After all, who promotes a joker?

Friend: Now thinking is joking?

Director: Jokes can spur thought. Whatever it takes.

Friend: And you really mean 'whatever'.

Director: Yes, whatever it takes for the sake of thought. For the active life. For life... at all.

57

Friend: So you'd be ruthless about thought?

Director: You make it sound like thought's a bad thing.

Friend: Would you be ruthless?

Director: Would I do whatever it takes for thought? Yes, I like to think I would. But I have a cowardly streak that stops me at times.

Friend: I don't believe you.

Director: It's up to me to decide whether I have it or not.

Friend: And if you decide you're cowardly?

Director: I have to compel myself to be brave.

Friend: How do you do that?

Director: I reason with myself. And when I come to the inescapable conclusion that thought is what counts in life, I ask myself how I can abandon the cause.

Friend: You shame yourself.

Director: I do. But not for long. It's never good to act too much out of shame. I find the positive reasons to act. And then I steel myself to act, though 'steel' is a little too strong.

Friend: I wish I could have such resolve.

Director: You can. You just need the reasons.

Friend: Where can I find them?

Director: We've gone over some of them today.

Friend: But I'll forget.

Director: Not the important things, you won't. But either way, I'd be happy to talk about this some more another time. Good things bear repeating. And who knows what we've missed?

Friend: That's a good point. Some people get upset if you bring something up you've already discussed. I think that's foolish. There's almost always something more, another angle to consider.

Director: Those other angles can be irritants.

Friend: True. Why do you think that is?

Director: People don't want to think. Other angles invite you to think.

Friend: People want to believe they know all there is to know.

Director: They certainly do. At least about certain things. They're happy to learn trivia and so on. In fact, some people spend great amounts of energy learning such things.

Friend: No doubt they do. And they consider themselves curious and mentally stimulated by these things. But I call it passivity.

Director: Are they mentally stimulated?

Friend: Their minds definitely get a workout. It's no small feat learning all the statistics in sports, for instance. But that's just memory, not thought.

Director: So we can exercise our memories to no good end?

Friend: I don't think it's necessarily bad to memorize statistics. But it is if it comes at the price of thought. And I think it often does.

Director: People often suppress their thoughts. And memories can be the means.

Friend: We should think about our memories, analyze them. Not live in them as if in a fog.

Director: You're going to run into fierce opposition here. Don't you know that people cherish their memories, even hold them sacred?

Friend: Well, for certain memories of course they should. I cherish the memories of my first cat. I don't know that I'd call them sacred, though. But bad memories have to go.

Director: I'm not sure anyone would argue with you there. Unless they say you should learn from those memories.

Friend: You should learn and then forget.

Director: Tell me. What does it mean to analyze a memory?

Friend: Here's an example. I used to think the way kids teased each other was fun. But now that I think about it, look back on my school years, I just think it was mean.

Director: So now you can forget you were mean? Now that you know?

Friend: I sounds bad to put it that way. Maybe I should remember, as a sort of punishment.

Director: Maybe. Or maybe you should act.

Friend: Think some more?

Director: Think some more and find the ones you teased.

Friend: They don't want to hear from me.

Director: Maybe you can learn something from them.

Friend: That's selfish, don't you think? Why bother them? Why not leave them alone?

Director: Leave them alone with their bad memories of school?

Friend: Alright, you have a point. It might be time to act and make new memories.

Director: Yes. But here's something important to know. When we think, we remember what we think.

Friend: Why is that important to know? I can remember the first time I thought a certain thing. So what?

Director: If what we thought proves true, we might want to share the thought.

Friend: Why is memory important for that?

Director: Our memory of the time before the thought might teach us to be patient, to be gentle. Some thoughts aren't easy to have.

Friend: That's very true. And the ones that aren't easy to have are the ones we remember most and best.

Director: There's a sort of victory in having such thoughts.

Friend: I couldn't agree with you more. And liberation, too. But what's the difference between having a thought and thinking?

Director: Are you wondering because someone can slip a thought in your ear, a thought that might make you think?

Friend: Yes. But I think I have my answer. Thoughts are the product of thinking.

Director: And knowledge?

Friend: Knowledge derives from thoughts working together to prove something true.

Director: You sound like a philosopher.

Friend: Thanks! I owe it all to you.

Director: I didn't do anything. You brought this out of yourself.

Friend: You really believe that?

Director: No, I know that.

Friend: But you gave me things to think about.

Director: And the thinking was done by you. That's the important fact in all this.

Friend: But some people are better at spurring thought than others.

Director: It's chemistry, Friend. I with most others spur no thought. But with my true friends? There's thought.

Friend: Chemistry. Chemistry makes for thought. Human chemistry is impossible to control. It's unpredictable.

Director: I'm not so sure. There's a science to chemistry. But it's very hard to learn. It takes lots and lots of experience, trial and error, and a determination to think.

Friend: Our chances for chemistry improve when we think?

Director: A thousand times over, yes. And thinking makes us more open to chemistry, too.

Friend: Who can resist chemistry?

Director: You might be surprised. Good things meet resistance every day. But chemistry is more precious than gold. You'd be a fool to let it slip away.

Friend: Just to be sure, we're not talking about romance, are we?

Director: We're talking about human connection, romantic or not. Chemistry doesn't lie. When it speaks to the heart, as friend, lover, acquaintance, stranger, whatever—we should listen. And then we should think.

Friend: I think it's hardest when we have chemistry with what we might call an enemy.

Director: There's certainly much to learn there. Many things to rethink. But remember, the other needs to be thinking, too.

Friend: What if they're not?

Director: The chemistry isn't full. Learn what you can and get out.

Friend: Why get out?

Director: So you can keep on searching for full chemistry, for friends.

Friend: Is anyone you have full chemistry with a friend?

Director: That's what I call them. But there are other names, depending.

Friend: Why can't you search for full while involved in halfway chemistry?

Director: Chemistry is draining when it's not full. Your expended energy won't be replenished.

Friend: It's like unrequited love.

Director: It's exactly like that. Learn and get out.

Friend: What if it takes you a long time to learn?

Director: Be sure you're actually learning and learn what you can. You'll know when you're getting diminishing returns.

Friend: Some people never know that.

Director: Some people are fools.

Friend: Can we go active-to-active with fools?

Director: Possibly. Again, it all depends.

Friend: What's a sure sign? And now that I'm thinking about it, is the sign always that we have chemistry? Is that what all active-to-active relationships are? Why didn't we say this from the start?

Director: Because then it wasn't clear. But there's a bit of a tricky question here. Can we be active because we have chemistry? Or do we feel chemistry because we're active? Who can say? But the two go together. Of that I'm sure.

58

Friend: Maybe chemistry is activity, and activity is chemistry.

Director: Maybe. It might be interesting to rehash our whole conversation substituting one for the other.

Friend: We should do it!

Director: Let's find a few friends and plan another night out.

Friend: That's an excellent idea. My, it's gotten late. We'd better get back.

Director: It has gotten late. I think we covered a lot of ground.

Friend: We did. And I think we were pretty active in the process.

Director: Process. So much in our world today has to do with process. Why do you think that is?

Friend: Science. Science relies on process. The scientific method is a process. Science has been so successful that we want to apply process to all aspects of our lives.

Director: I don't.

Friend: Neither do I. What does that make us?

Director: Active.

Friend: Ha, ha! It's true! You can fall asleep in process, put it on autopilot. Take process away and almost everyone is lost.

Director: How can we take process away?

Friend: Get people to think outside the box.

Director: The box is process?

Friend: Yes, or method, or whatever. It's a predefined way of dealing with reality. But reality doesn't like being predefined. We have to take it as it comes and think accordingly, not shove it in some box.

Director: But the box promises many good things.

Friend: And we can take those things, but step out from time to time.

Director: The box won't get jealous?

Friend: Well, maybe it will. Or those who never leave the box will. In fact, I'm certain they will.

Director: What can we do?

Friend: Not make a scene of our leaving the box.

Director: Leave the box in secret?

Friend: Not wholly. We let those with chemistry in on our way.

Director: 'Way' is different than 'process', isn't it?

Friend: It certainly is. I think way and chemistry are related.

Director: If we follow our chemistry we follow our way.

Friend: Yes! That's exactly it. No box, however strong, can keep chemistry away.

Director: That's where I'm not sure, Friend. I can imagine a box that's very, very strong indeed. A box that very well might snuff out life.

Friend: What, like some science fiction horror?

Director: Or worse. It's not enough to follow chemistry. We have to deal with the box, the passive-making box.

Friend: Is there an activity box?

Director: I think the idea of box precludes that notion. But maybe I'm wrong. It would take a long conversation to see, I think.

Friend: Let's take that up another time.

Director: Let's.

Friend: But I can't help wondering more about our way, and whether it's not enough to follow it.

Director: We have to deal with the passive-making box. But I'm not sure if we have to go out of our way to do it. I am sure, however, that if it gets in the way we must deal with it at once.

Friend: Why at once? Why not fall back and regroup with a plan?

Director: That's not a bad idea. But there's a temptation to keep falling back, and back, and make plans that never get executed in full. That's why I'm inclined to deal with it at once.

Friend: To stay on your way.

Director: To stay on my way. And if I get overwhelmed? Then I'll fall back and regroup.

Friend: I think that's a very good approach. I only hope I have the courage a plan like that requires.

Director: Just follow your way. And be rightly upset when someone stands in it.

Friend: Because we have a right to our way.

Director: Not exactly. Maybe I shouldn't have said 'rightly'.

Friend: What should you have said?

Director: Stir yourself when someone stands in your way. And do whatever you have to do to keep on keeping on.

Friend: I agree. And I take it you really mean we have to do whatever it takes, absolutely whatever.

Director: Absolutely whatever, yes. But I don't mean shoot the person. That won't put you back on your way.

Friend: Why wouldn't it?

Director: It will land you in jail.

Friend: Of course. I see what you mean. So you don't really mean absolutely whatever.

Director: No, I do mean absolutely whatever. Just don't do things that won't put you on your way, like whatever would send you to jail. And so on.

Friend: Okay. I understand.

Director: Good. While the way is one, we all have different ways.

Friend: Can we help another get on their way?

Director: Yes and no. Yes we can suggest that they might be missing an opportunity to get on their way, and they'll take it from there. But they have to take it from there. It's all up to them.

Friend: At best suggestions. But suggestions can be much.

Director: True, we can help each other in this world. But telling a yet-to-run great runner, 'Hey, I think you can run,' doesn't make them run.

Friend: Are you saying we deserve no credit for our suggestions?

Director: Maybe a little, as in being known as perspicacious. But more than that? No.

Friend: Doesn't the 'runner' owe you thanks?

Director: Not really. I would just love to see them run. That's thanks enough for me.

Friend: Are you selfless?

Director: No! The selfless don't think. The selfless cannot think.

Friend: Why not?

Director: Because thinking supposes an 'I'.

Friend: I thought philosophy would question the 'I'.

Director: Philosophy does. What is the 'I'? I've asked myself this a thousand times. But each time 'I' asks 'me'. I can't see a way around it. Can you?

Friend: Who, me?

Director: Yes you. Can you? Please tell me if you can.

Friend: But I can't!

Director: That's alright. Maybe one day we'll find someone who can.

Friend: But, seriously, why would you even want to find a way around it?

Director: Because it's the biggest assumption we make.

Friend: But what about chemistry? There is no chemistry without an 'I'.

Director: Maybe. But then again, maybe there is.

Friend: What, some sort of collective chemistry?

Director: I just don't know. It's a nagging question.

Friend: Well, stop worrying about it. The self-evident 'I' will always be there.

Director: Always? Even with the convergence of biotechnology and artificial intelligence? Are you sure?

Friend: No, I'm not sure.

Director: Then we'd better try to give it some thought whenever we can. The stakes are high, very high—perhaps the highest yet.

59

Friend: You're so serious.

Director: Would you like me to joke about this?

Friend: No, I take it seriously, too.

Director: Rethinking the 'I' can be very heavy work.

Friend: Won't it just happen naturally as we advance in technology?

Director: Why would it?

Friend: I... don't know. Tell me something. Are you in favor of Babel?

Director: As in the Tower of Babel? In order to stop technology's progress?

Friend: Yes.

Director: It doesn't matter. It's not up to me.

Friend: You're taking the easy way out.

Director: Then you tell me. How could I stop technology's progress? Babel aside.

Friend: You could call the progress passive, and explain yourself to those in the know. That would be a start.

Director: Progress can be passive?

Friend: Don't play dumb. Of course it can. It's a process. 'Progress' has dug a deep rut. And it will just go on and on, digging ever deeper. Until we can never get out of the canyon.

Director: Then let's make technologists think.

Friend: They already think they think.

Director: Do they think about these sorts of things? Or do they think about getting promoted for discovering better tools, winning patents, and so on?

Friend: Don't forget about getting rich.

Director: Yes, they may think about that most of all. But that's very narrow thinking, don't you think?

Friend: I agree. They may only be active in ten degrees out of three-hundred-and-sixty. They need to do more.

Director: If the 'I' is to survive.

Friend: I think that's what's at stake.

Director: Then we know who to talk to next.

Friend: But how? You're resigning from work, where you had access to some of these people.

Director: I'll just have to find a way to do it on my own. And you?

Friend: I'll make friends and talk to them about this.

Director: Good. That's how it starts. I'll do the same.

Friend: But what if I have no chemistry with them? I haven't up until now.

Director: We have to count on some luck. That's how these things work. So never let a chance slip.

Friend: I promise I won't. How often do chances occur?

Director: Sometimes only once in a lifetime.

Friend: That's a very serious thing.

Director: But listen to us. Can we really make them think? They have to do it on their own.

Friend: Yes but we can give them something to think about. Then they may or may not think.

Director: If there's chemistry chances are good they will.

Friend: Exactly. But didn't we say chemistry is thought?

Director: We may or may not be right about that.

Friend: Let's call it a hypothesis to be tested when we can.

Director: An excellent idea. We'll go on a hunt for chemistry and see if we think.

Friend: And we'll see if we have chemistry every time we think. But wait. This makes no sense.

Director: Why not? What have you found?

Friend: How could we have forgotten we think when we're alone!

Director: But don't you know?

Friend: Know what?

Director: We can have chemistry with ourselves.

Friend: We can?

Director: Of course we can! Haven't you ever heard of being a friend to yourself?

Friend: I thought when people said they're their own best friend it was just a figure of speech.

Director: For many I'm sure it is. But for people like us it's very real.

Friend: How can it be real for me if I don't even know what it means?

Director: I have experience spotting self-friendship and I see it latent in you.

Friend: What do I need to do to bring it out? Trust my feelings and act on them?

Director: Think on them, yes. Then once you've thought, do something. Then see what you think about that.

Friend: And the chemistry is all in there somewhere?

Director: Yes. I haven't been able to locate it exactly. Maybe you will and can teach me.

Friend: You really think so?

Director: That's my hope.

Friend: You place hope on me?

Director: I place hope on all my friends. That's one of the reasons they're my friends.

Friend: They want to be your friends because you place hope on them, or you want to be friends with them because they make you hopeful?

Director: Exactly. Both. Do you still want to be my friend?

Friend: Of course! You make me hopeful, too.

Director: What do you hope?

Friend: That I'll figure something out about chemistry and thought. I really want to know.

Director: That makes two of us. The flame.

Friend: Yes, the flame of knowledge!

Director: People often talk about the torch of knowledge. But I like flame better. Fire out of nowhere, you know?

Friend: I do know. And I like it, too.

Director: But what are we saying? The flame must come from somewhere, if we're totally honest.

Friend: We should be honest. The flame comes from experience and thought.

Director: Which is the spark and which the fuel?

Friend: That's an interesting question. I think thought is the spark and experience the fuel.

Director: So in order to know something we must keep adding experience as fuel.

Friend: It sounds a little strange but I think it's true. The experience keeps confirming what we know.

Director: Or causes us to adjust.

Friend: To refine our knowledge, yes.

Director: And sometimes it's more than a refinement. Sometimes it's an overhaul.

Friend: But if that's the case how could we have had a flame? Do you know what I'm asking?

Director: I think I do. Maybe it's just a false light.

Friend: What does that mean?

Director: Maybe we're seeing the light through a filter. And when we learn the truth we see the pure light.

Friend: Maybe. But it still doesn't sound right.

Director: I think it's because of the limit of the metaphor.

Friend: Of course. These things aren't that easy.

Director: Metaphors can shed some light, but only some. It's tempting to take them too far. So tempting, in fact, I'm tempted never to use them.

Friend: Then you can't speak the language because language is loaded with metaphors.

Director: You're right. So what can we do?

Friend: Take it all with a grain of salt.

Director: Don't be too serious.

Friend: Yes. When you say knowledge is a flame, I nod and agree but have my reservations.

Director: But why be reserved? Why not share your reservations?

Friend: With you I will, and have. But many people, when confronted with an assertion, are afraid to qualify that assertion, let alone disagree.

Director: Why do you think that is?

Friend: They want to be liked. They're afraid how the other will react. They're lazy. You pick which one it is.

Director: Probably some toxic brew of the three. But all three can be countered by self-respect.

Friend: That's exactly true. If you respect yourself, you don't care if you're liked. If you respect yourself, you don't care how the other will react. And if you respect yourself, you won't let laziness determine your course. Respect and activity go hand in hand.

Director: I think we're on to something here. What's the opposite of respect?

Friend: Disrespect?

Director: Do people disrespect themselves, or have we got the wrong word?

Friend: No, I think we can disrespect ourselves.

Director: Do we actively disrespect ourselves?

Friend: Never. Disrespect is a passive thing.

Director: Self-disrespect only, or the disrespect of others, too?

Friend: I think it gets confusing here.

Director: Why?

Friend: Through activity you might be perceived as being disrespectful.

Director: But you're only perceived, not actually so?

Friend: I'm... not sure.

Director: Who perceives activity as disrespectful?

Friend: The passive.

Director: Are you sure?

Friend: Positive.

Director: Is the activity truly disrespectful?

Friend: Only to those propped up by lies.

Director: That's an interesting turn.

Friend: It's the truth.

Director: Passivity and lies go hand in hand?

Friend: It's easier to lie than tell the truth.

Director: What makes the truth so hard?

Friend: It's often inconvenient. And it requires explanation and demonstration, both of which are activities.

Director: Yes, I think that makes good sense. But isn't it hard to maintain a lie? Didn't we talk a bit about this before?

Friend: We did. But that's the irony. Liars think it's easy to lie. But all the lies take their toll. In the end it might be harder to lie than tell the truth.

Director: Try and convince the lazy to speak the truth for the sake of their ease!

Friend: I know, it sounds crazy. But it's the long term versus the short term view.

Director: That sounds very wise. I'll make it my policy to tell the truth.

Friend: Don't tease. I'm serious.

Director: And so am I.

60

Friend: Is there anything about passivity we haven't touched upon?

Director: I'd say we've made a good start.

Friend: Start? We've said so much!

Director: But there's much more that can be said. A philosopher might make many comments on our conversation. In fact, for every five minutes of talk I think the philosopher could fill a volume.

Friend: That's a lot of volumes. Do you think people would read them?

Director: Stranger things have happened. You never really know what's going to capture someone's attention.

Friend: It's a matter of chemistry, isn't it? But you said there's a science to chemistry.

Director: If a philosopher writes with a particular person in mind, there can be a science.

Friend: But what about a particular type of person?

Director: The science there is less exact.

Friend: But possible.

Director: Yes.

Friend: I would rather write for a type.

Director: Why?

Friend: There's a better chance of success.

Director. But what if the person you write for is representative of a type?

Friend: Like the type 'active'?

Director: Usually more of a mixed type, active and passive. You'll have no purchase with the purely passive. And there's really no such thing as a purely active person.

Friend: But then there's no such thing as a purely passive person, is there?

Director: A good point. Then we should think in terms of percentage active or passive. Where would you aim?

Friend: Fifty-fifty. And you?

Director: Ninety-ten.

Friend: Ninety percent active?

Director: Why no. Passive.

Friend: Why aim so low?

Director: Low? Do you have any idea how hard it is to find someone ten percent active? Haven't you looked around?

Friend: I thought you were aiming for the one.

Director: In other things, yes. But when it comes to what I'd write? Ten is a good place to aim.

Friend: I don't believe you. I think you'd find a way to write for both the ten and your one at once.

Director: How would I do that?

Friend: Your writing would say different things to different people. It would be layered in meaning.

Director: I wish I could do what you say. But then again, every piece of writing says different things to different people. People bring their experience to bear in their interpretation of the written word. And everyone's experience is different. No?

Friend: True. But two tens will have more similar experience with each other than either would with a five. No?

Director: That's likely true, if we're talking about significant experience.

Friend: Say more about what you mean by 'significant'.

Director: I could grow up in the same town as a five, as you put it, and have lots of common experience. But a ten—assuming I too am a ten—from another country would have more in common with me, more meaningful things in common with me, than my hometown five.

Friend: So you write about hometown things in a way that speaks both to the five and ten.

Director: You might be on to something here.

Friend: You find the universal in the local. That's the trick!

Director: I'm not so sure about the 'universal'.

Friend: Why not?

Director: Universals are an easy way out from thought. Thought is in the particular.

Friend: But what about ideas?

Director: Ideas don't have to be universal.

Friend: I've never heard of a particular idea.

Director: Maybe it's time to think about it. And I'm sure you've heard about particular ideas. Haven't you ever heard someone say, 'I have a great idea!'

Friend: Of course I have. But that's not the kind of idea I meant.

Director: You meant some eternal, general idea.

Friend: Yes.

Director: The time for those is gone. Or perhaps put better, such ideas are dead.

Friend: Who killed them?

Director: We did.

Friend: How so?

Director: What gives life to ideas?

Friend: People believing in them

Director: Well, people no longer believe in them. It's as simple as that. Isn't it?

Friend: Yes, but they should.

Director: Why?

Friend: Because ideas give us something in common.

Director: I thought tens will have something in common with tens. And twenties will have something in common with twenties. And so on, and so on.

Friend: Yes, but twenties need something in common with tens.

Director: Why?

Friend: To keep the peace!

Director: They can have their home towns in common. And so on, and so on.

Friend: I think you're missing the point.

Director: What's the point?

Friend: We need ideas that lift us up.

Director: To where?

Friend: What do you mean?

Director: Where shall we be lifted?

Friend: Above the petty, the provincial. You know.

Director: We'll be lifted up to grand ideas. But I'm not sure how much good grand ideas have done. In fact, I'm fairly certain they're the cause of a whole lot of trouble.

Friend: Why do you think that?

Director: Idea clashes with idea.

Friend: That's why we need to be on the same page.

Director: Throughout the whole world?

Friend: Yes!

Director: That would be quite a trick. I'd rather not see it done.

Friend: But this way everyone might become a hundred, fully active in thought! Wouldn't you like to see that?

Director: I'm not sure what you think is possible is possible. Plus I'm scared.

Friend: Scared of billions of hundreds? Why?

Director: Because it might prove thought isn't as good as we think. And that would turn our world upside down.

Friend: Well, I'm sure you're up for it! Let's strive for that.

Director: For rethinking the world? Okay, I'm game. But I want you to think, too. Keep me company.

Friend: I will. It's only fair. So are we done?

Director: With our dialogue tonight? We're done. I'm left with a rethinking of everything I know. And you're left with, what? Some general promise to think?

Friend: That's a good thing to be left with. I'm sure you agree.

Director: I agree. But I'll press you on the particulars.

Friend: That's the kind of pressure I can live with. And I'll press you on the general. I think you're going to come up with some very good ideas.

Director: With your prompting, I won't be surprised if we do.

Friend: 'We'? You're the big thinker.

Director: If I am it's because I have to be. But you're the real man of ideas.

Friend: Thank you. But I'll remember your caution about ideas.

Director: Should we issue a caution about thinking, too?

Friend: What caution does it need?

Director: I'm not sure. I thought you might know.

Friend: The only caution here is for the passive.

Director: Why the passive?

Friend: Because thinking will turn their world upside down!

Director: Okay. But what about the active? Can they throw caution to the wind?

Friend: The active will know when caution is due.

Director: And when it's due, they'll think with great care?

Friend: The greatest, yes.

Director: Then with that let's end our talk. But we'll do it again. And next time, with friends.

Printed in the United States
by Baker & Taylor Publisher Services